*Healing the Wound
from My Daughter's Suicide*

Healing the Wound from My Daughter's Suicide

GRIEF TRANSLATED INTO WORDS

Lois Severson

iUniverse, Inc.
Bloomington

HEALING THE WOUND FROM MY DAUGHTER'S SUICIDE
GRIEF TRANSLATED INTO WORDS

iUniverse books may be ordered through booksellers or by contacting:

iUniverse
1663 Liberty Drive
Bloomington, IN 47403
www.iuniverse.com
1-800-Authors (1-800-288-4677)

ISBN: 978-1-4759-8932-8 (sc)
ISBN: 978-1-4759-8934-2 (hc)
ISBN: 978-1-4759-8933-5 (e)

Library of Congress Control Number: 2013907983

Printed in the United States of America.

iUniverse rev. date: 5/15/2013

April 29, 1979

Patty now lives life in a form we cannot see

Dedication

In memory of
Patty

With all our LOVE

Bob, Lois, and Jeanne

Table of Contents

Acknowledgements

Donna Amick-Anderson
Bob and Jeanne
Fr. Brian Beno
Cathy Berg
Mary Brennan
Donna Danowski
Nik Dubois
Kathleen Johnston
Becky Murray
Jacquelyn Oliveira
Fr. Ron Rolheiser, OMI
Fran and Tom Smith
Sister Virginia Stone
Lynn Woehlke
Class of '60
Local Loises
Metro Bible Study Companions
My Family
My Friends
All Who Listened

Prologue

June 23, 2005, 9:45 AM

Last night, while all of us were doing our routine, a dear friend of ours left for the unknown. No explanation. No signs. Nothing. Everything appeared to be the norm, and would continue as is. However, there is a void that is present in all of our hearts and souls.

Patty was always a person that made whatever event a pleasant one: summer nights at Fat Daddy's playing volleyball in the sand, spring and fall Saturdays playing on the football field of battle, weekend jaunts to the North woods for rafting, more volleyball and conversation. Whatever it was, she always made it fun to be there.

Her smile was infectious. Her love for the people in her life was always known and easily seen, whether it was that smile, a quick hug or her resting her head on your shoulder. Her caring instinct for everyone came through whenever we were injured, physically or emotionally. She always had two arms, two shoulders and one big heart for all those in her life who needed someone at whatever time.

All of us have questions that cannot be answered. All of us want to know the why. All of us have to bond together and keep her spirit alive in us. She may have physically left us, but she will always be with us: smiling when we do, hugging us when we're sad.

A very important part of our routine is now missing. This has hit us all the same, with different results and emotional responses. But everyone needs to take comfort in the fact that Patty will always be there for us, just in spirit, and we have to accept that and welcome it at the same time. It may seem as though nothing will ever be the same, and it won't. But we have to accept it. It will take time.

Our routine continues...

~Nik
(Friend of Patty's)

Introduction

*"Give sorrow words: the
Grief that does not speak
Whispers the o'er-fraught
Heart and bids it break."*
William Shakespeare's Macbeth, Act IV, Scene 3

I f you are reading this, it is probably because a relative or friend was a victim of suicide. You have been shaken in your boots and are wondering when the earthquake will stop. Our family has been in your shoes. There is no simple way to express the pain and anguish such an experience exudes. I do not pretend to be an authority on suicide, but I do have experience as a griever. The purpose of this book is to share that grief experience with you. Why share?

*"I hear and I forget; I see and I remember; I write
and I understand." Chinese Proverb*

As this proverb indicates, translating my grief into words helps me understand and consequently heals my wound. I would make the same recommendation to any griever: write, write, write. As in Scripture I am using the word three times for emphasis and to indicate a transition to something *new* during the grief process. Constant writing will unveil that *newness* when it happens.

Seven years have passed since our twenty-six year old daughter, Patty, was a victim of suicide. The pain has not gone away but I think it is different somehow. Something changed in me between the sixth and seventh anniversary. The sixth anniversary was very difficult because every day of significance related to Patty's death happened on the same day of the week. It was reliving what had happened all over again in 2011. My sister, Anne, also had died two weeks before the anniversary. Anne was Patty's godmother and died at the same time of day as Patty had. I interpreted this as a sign that Patty was present for Anne's transition. That comforted me. I noticed that the writing for this book became a little easier. Prior to this I either wrote with emotion in a journal, not knowing if I should share the content with anyone. Or during my morning meditations I would wait for the urgency of the Spirit in prayer to write down ideas on scrap paper as they came to me.

As I wandered in my desert of grief from insight to insight, there were periods of drinking from God's stream and words would flow and ideas gel. I would write then with some efficiency. Perhaps my healing journey is nearing an end. It has been seven years of struggle in mind and soul to discern if this book should be. I always told myself: *If it is to be, somehow God will make it happen.* If the book is not complete by my time of death, I ask others to publish my testament of our family's experience. Some things I am writing about because I hope medical researchers will document them for future study of suicide. It should also help psychologists to note some of the facts involved.

In some areas of the book I simply want to explain how I found comfort and serenity in meditation. I beg you to get in touch with your own spirituality. It will save you, your mind and body. Somewhere I have read the expression that spirituality takes off where religion ends. I take this to be analogous to the Beatitudes going beyond the Ten Commandments. Religion may help us discover our spirituality, but once we develop it, we go beyond religion and find peace in investigating concepts such as suicide and resurrection where religion is deficient. In this light if you do not have faith to rely on or develop, I would suggest that you try *to* be aware that your suicide victim now exists in Spirit form. From the venue of your loved one's Spirit presence, re-enforce the love you have for your loved one, believing the bond of love still exists between yourself and the suicide victim. I believe your loved one may help you develop some faith or meaning in something or someone.

Hoping to be a trustworthy steward, my purpose in this writing is to share my thoughts and feelings with those who were not able to prevent the suicide of a loved one. Even though my grieving may be different than yours, my hope is that my expression of grief may help you express yours. It is extremely healthy to get your grief out in the open and not keep it pent up inside you.

In the first months after our Patty died, I went to bed each evening reading other people's stories of suicide, experiences they shared, and facts about suicide. This helped my mind settle down to know we were not alone in this "suicide soup." I use that expression because that is what it felt like at first: like we were swimming around in some chaotic sea, swirling from place to place, trying to make sense out of what we were doing in the aftermath. Our experience with suicide and my reading have certainly indicated that there is mystery surrounding this kind of death, even when a note is left. I will try to address that idea in Chapter 7. Because I do not have all the answers, I ask God for His guidance in accomplishing this task. I do not write from a self-defensive position. I can only enter the suicide arena with softness, compassion, and the realization that I am speaking of a treasure God has put in my lap. May I be the steward He wants me to be.

As you read, remember everyone grieves differently so I am not preaching: "Do it my way." I believe the sharing of reactions and responses helps both the writer and the reader. Certainly pick and choose as determined by your needs. I found in my early reading that certain sections of books popped out at me and to these I gave my attention.

Obviously, another main reason for this writing is my hope of promoting more understanding of mental illness and to "break the silence" on suicide. Chapter six gets into the blindness we all exhibit in these areas.

At first I tried to cross check in my writing for repetition from chapter to chapter. Later, I decided not to delete repetitions because I remembered that people need to hear things six times to remember them and then only remember ten percent of that.

This writing should provide a forum to have discussions on suicide and death. Our society needs this forum because many people fear such a discussion. I am so proud of my husband. Even though he is less expressive with his grief, he still listens to me when I express mine, and he participates in that discussion when I bring things up. I have discovered that the reason fifty percent of the couples who lose a child divorce is because each of them grieves so differently. One woman told me their divorce was precipitated by one partner wanting to stay in the house they had when their daughter died and the other partner could not tolerate living in the house any longer. So I greatly appreciate being able to talk to my husband about Patty and about suicide. We all need to comfort and console each other.

Suicide is definitely an arena in which everyone has an opinion. In expressing that opinion I believe one should withhold moral judgment. No one but God can be an authority in that department. Do not play the blame game: blame the victim (selfish); blame self (guilt over what could have been done); blame others (least line of resistance). These are ways of poisoning one's own mind. Instead face reality: the pattern of life has death in it. Remember that the minute we are born, the count-down to our death begins. Perhaps we find death difficult to discuss because it makes us think of our own death. We would rather pretend everything will go on as usual. The fact that the death may have been suicide does complicate the issue. But as humans we cannot grasp all its meaning. It becomes one of those questions we live each day.

First, we need to keep in mind that the suicide is not about us; it is about our loved one: the great gift of him/her in our lives. Secondly, suicide is a no more shameful death than death caused by cancer, kidney disease, or a heart attack. In fact, suicide is a mind attack. Just like a heart attack, the mind attack affects a real part of the body: the brain (where decisions are made).

A mental health disorder is a disease of the brain, a biological malfunction of the brain. Just as some of the physical diseases mentioned above are curable, likewise some mental health disorders can be fixed by a combination of therapy and medications. Therapists emphasize both are necessary. But just as some cancer treatments are not successful, so some mental health disorders are not treated successfully. Just as some cancers take the life of their victims, so do some brain disorders take the life of their victims in what we call suicide. Not all cancers are curable. Not all suicides can be prevented.

Just as one learns to accept the death of a loved one struck by cancer, so one can learn to accept the death of a loved one struck by suicide. Society and religion have trouble with this notion and so label such victims as "not normal." I have trouble with this label because our daughter, Patty, wore a mask of "normal." Many said so and were shocked at her manner of death. Yes, she had some "baggage" but everyone I know has some "baggage." All humans do. That's what makes us human. It has led me to believe that all of us have a bit of "abnormal." As we go through life we perceive our own abnormalities, accept them, attempt to fix them, and become a better person.

When a loved one is a victim of suicide, he/she has not been able to fix his/her abnormalities, feels helpless and hopeless, and gives up the human struggle to fix and repair. This helplessness is what touches me the most in the suicide of our daughter. This helplessness is what should touch society and religions when another suicide is announced. This "helplessness" creates an arena of compassion for our human condition, not an arena of shame, discontent, or unspeakable evil.

As this book focuses on a healing acceptance of a loved one's suicide by acknowledging that our "loved one" is all right in resurrection form, my hope is that you will also be all right as you discover a new identity as a suicide survivor. This new identity should unveil an "open heart" full of understanding, poured out to accept one's situation and surroundings.

Most often people need to experience the suicide of a person close to them to really work at understanding the situation with compassion.

The personal experience puts a whole different spin on the word and its significance. The hurt and the pain pries open our eyes and minds.

The relief I experienced reading accounts of suicide and instructional material on the subject probably stemmed from the fact that society and religion had hidden that world from me by the shunning, dismissing, hiding, and denying deaths by suicide.

If you are reading this book and think suicide will not touch your life, think again. One tends to think that it only happens to other people. I perhaps thought that way once. I never would have predicted suicide would happen in our little family of four. I somehow knew a great suffering was coming in my life in the future but had no idea it would be our daughter's suicide at age twenty-six. So another point I wish to make is: suicide can touch anyone. I am a witness to that. With over thirty-seven thousand known suicides in the U.S. each year, it is very possible you have already been touched and do not even know it because of people's denial. The silence about suicide needs to be broken. It is like the elephant in the room that no one wants to talk about. But it is present. It exists. It really happens. Suicide is a permanent solution to a temporary problem. Families intimately touched by it should not feel shame. They should feel free to admit, not deny, what has happened to them.

We should publicize every suicide because each suicide is a reminder that all is not well with the world. It would be interesting to know how many families were touched by suicide if the truth was always told. I would hypothesize that almost every family tree has one or more in its branches.

As much as we would like things to go on as usual, they will not. We discover that principle in our grief process as we change. We will never be the same again. Our identity has permanently changed. Part of our grief process involves recognizing and assessing that new identity. Then we have to decide how we will live with that new identity.

Last, but not least, I want to give credit to mothers I know who are aware of their children's handicaps: physical, emotional, or mental. I want to encourage these mothers to endure, persevere, and never give up being your child's advocate. Our society needs to get over labeling differences as weaknesses. We all have "differences" if we are honest with ourselves. It is our job to support each other in our human frailty. Are suicides a reflection of all human frailty?

The methods used by suicide victims to transition to the next stage of life are startling events that should awaken all humanity, sharpen our perception of values that matter, and lead to a changed way of living for those closely touched by their lives. I pray that this book will provide some shepherding, direction, guidance, and hope for those who are surviving a suicide experience. Every person can be comfortable processing grief in their own way. Be kind to yourself. Treat yourself gently.

Be at Peace
Do not look forward in fear
To the changes in life;
Rather, look to them with full hope
That as they arise, God,
Whose very own you are,
Will lead you safely through all things;
And when you cannot stand it,
God will carry you in His Arms.
Do not fear what may happen tomorrow;
The same understanding Father
Who cares for you today
Will take care of you then and every day.
He will either shield you from suffering
Or give you unfailing strength to bear it.
Be at peace, and put aside all
Anxious thoughts and imaginations.
(St. Francis de Sales)

Chapter 1

Shock of our Lives

"...he has sent me... to heal the
brokenhearted, to proclaim liberty
to the captives and release to the
prisoners." Isaiah 61:1-2a, 10-11

*On June 22, 2005 Patty was healed of her brokenness, no longer
held captive in this life, and released from her imprisoned mind.*

For two years before Patty died, I would frequently get mind pictures of Patty coming out of her bedroom sobbing hysterically and panicking over the fact that she did not hear her alarm clock and would now be late for work. I assumed I pictured this because Patty was always overtired, had trouble going to sleep because of anxiety, and then could hardly wake up to the alarm once she finally got to sleep. The irony here is that we believe this is what she experienced before her last panic attack which led to her suicide on June 22, 2005 at five in the afternoon. From her boy friend we learned Patty had not slept June 19th and 20th. Yet she had worked all day June 20th and 21st at her new first shift position in surgery. The nurse who worked with her June 21st said Patty had been focused that day. Another lady who saw her at lunch that day said Patty looked sad. (A friend saw her at the bank on her way home from work that day and said Patty looked sad).

I was also told by hospital staff that she drank lots of caffeine drinks at work like Red Bull and had Stay Awake pills in her work locker. Being so sleep deprived she must have taken two diazepam in order to sleep the night of June 21st after she called her dad at Elmbrook Hospital. Diazepam is a generic form of valium which makes panic attacks worse and can even cause panic attacks when you are coming off of it. We found two diazepam wrappers (each five mg) on her night stand and one for alprazolam (one-fourth mg), a sleeping tablet. After investigation, it seems that Patty slept through her entire day of work. Her new cell phone had two calls from the hospital: one at seven-thirty in the morning and another one at two-thirty in the afternoon. (It bothered me that the hospital never called us in the afternoon when they got no answer the second time. We were listed as her emergency contact). A month later I learned that Patty's neighbor across the hall told the police she had seen Patty at three in the afternoon and she had looked sad. We think she thought she would be terminated from the hospital for missing the day of work and panicked. Patty never tried to call any of us, wrote a suicide note, put a sticky note on her driver's license that said, "Call my mom and dad," and gave our phone number. With driver's license in hand, she jumped out her living room window (from the sixth floor). She landed on the ground about twenty feet from the swimming pool. No one at the pool witnessed the jump. One gentleman there said there was no sound. The doctor who did the autopsy said she died upon impact due to excessive bleeding in the heart-lung area. Her heart was literally smashed. All her limbs were fractured multiple times and bones punctured the skin. Her clothes were bloody. Spinal fluid was coming out of her nose. When Vince and Katerina got to her side, at four fifty-five, Katerina, a nurse, could not get a pulse. It seemed so unbelievable that such a gentle, compassionate person could die in such a way. Patty was declared dead at five twenty-one. Three weeks later after putting this timeline together, I could not help but think what I could have done with that time between two-thirty and five o'clock, since most suicide books say the impulsivity or the "temporarily insane" time for the suicide victim is most often ten to fifteen minutes. But I did not let my thinking go there in 2005 because I knew what the reality was. All the hindsight in the world was not going to bring Patty back to this life with us.

I bear the heart ache that Patty did not call me as her last resort. I wanted to be there for her. I brought her into this world, but I could not be there as she left this world. I tell myself that God knows best even though I would rather give my life for hers. But God did send a nurse to hold Patty's hand as she went through her transition and transformation to the next stage of life.

Ironically during the time Patty was dying, Bob and I were at a free financial-planning dinner at Davian's. We were explaining to the people we ate dinner with that our daughter, Patty, had worked here cutting wedding cakes and waiting on tables for weddings when she was in high school to earn college tuition money. On our drive home from that dinner (about six-thirty in the evening), Jeanne, Patty's sister, called us frantically telling us that Patty's boy friend, Steve, had called her and was worried because every time he called Patty's phone number, the Cudahy police answered. The first time it happened the police simply would not tell him anything. Steve thought maybe someone had stolen Patty's cell phone again. (The week before someone broke into Patty's car to steal her cell phone and car radio). The second time Steve called Patty's phone number, the police answered again. This time they asked him who he was. He answered that he was Patty's boy friend and was worried about her. They then asked Steve if Patty had been depressed. He did not think so. Steve told us later that he never saw this coming in his relationship with Patty. Hospital workers told us the same thing. Her sister, Jeanne, had no indication of anxiety or depression either.

When Jeanne had reached us by cell phone, we were five minutes from home. She told me the Cudahy police told Steve that they would only talk to Patty's parents. We quickly drove home. As soon as I called the non-emergency number of the Cudahy police, I gave my name and reason for calling. The lady told me she would get the officer in charge of that case, which seemed to take forever. When that officer finally got to the phone, he verified my name, address and phone number.

When I questioned the officer about what happened, he responded that he was not allowed to tell me on the phone but would send an officer to our address and discussed what the closest police department might be. I offered to travel to the Cudahy Police Department and he said, "No," very emphatically. This was my clue that Patty was dead. Otherwise I assumed he would have directed us to a hospital.

It seemed like a nightmare waiting for the police, our agony in the garden. Bob found himself hoping Patty had been abducted so that some hope would remain that she was still alive. Later, he said, "How horrible is that?" His mind most likely went in that direction because the police in Aruba were still looking for Natalie Holloway.

While we waited for the police to come to our house, I stood in front of Patty's high school graduation picture and said to her in my mind: *I know you are dead and you are right here in Spirit. You have to let me know every day of my life that you are okay and happy.* I do think she started to do this right away as we made decisions in regard to her death. She helped me think clearly so I could ask the right questions of the right people that evening and the next day.

That agonizing wait took three hours. In the meantime our daughter Jeanne called several times to find out if we had any information yet. Finally a police car circled the subdivision and was checking addresses. We ran out on the porch and waved to him and he kept on driving. We called Cudahy police again; they were upset no one had shown up at our house yet. Another half hour elapsed because the inexperienced policeman was waiting for the Waukesha County chaplain to accompany him to deliver the news.

Finally they arrived at our front door. The policeman said: "Your daughter, Patty, is dead. It was suicide." I immediately asked, "How?" When he responded that she had jumped out a window, I had to cover my face so I could make a horrible face of pain and anguish; it seemed so awful and unimaginable. But I felt it important to ask the right questions at the right time for investigation purposes. So I continued,

"Which window?" The officer replied that I would have to call the medical examiner and gave me her phone number.

I left the two officers with Bob and immediately went to call the medical examiner. I was not frantic, not screaming, and not crying. After the three hours of waiting, I needed to get accurate information. The medical examiner told me Patty jumped out of the living room window, asked me some questions, mentioned the diazepam, oxycontin, and cyclobenzaprine prescriptions in the medicine cabinet, and gave me directions to the Milwaukee County morgue to come downtown and identify Patty. I told her we would be there as soon as we could physically make the trip. I quickly called Jeanne and gave her the news over the phone because she had been waiting so long. This was awful for her. I hated to make her wait any longer. But I wish that I had waited to be physically present to give her the news. Jeanne screamed and threw herself on the sidewalk in front of her condo on Water Street. Her boy friend had to carry her inside.

In the above call to Jeanne I asked her to call Patty's boy friend, Steve, and tell him. Again I should have done this myself, considering how young Jeanne and Steve were for something so traumatic. Steve's parents were very wise and went to Chicago to pick him up and brought him home to Hartford.

Before leaving the house for the morgue, I had to practice saying, "Patty is dead," out loud three times so I could get used to the sound of that reality, realizing I would have to say it often to inform others.

Bob and I drove to Jeanne's condo, picked her up, and drove to the morgue, arriving there about eleven in the evening. On the drive over to the morgue, Jeanne said, "How could Patty be so selfish?" I replied, "I don't think she was ever selfish. I think, in a sense, it was unselfish of her not to want to bother us anymore with her anxiety."

The medical examiner recommended identifying Patty by photo. At the death scene she had taken three head shots of Patty. She showed us these as well as a copy of the note Patty had written. I was relieved at the photos as Patty's face looked very peaceful. Her hair looked oily to indicate she had just awakened. (She had to wash her hair every morning because of the oiliness in it after sleep). When I got to the part of her note that said: "Please forgive me. I love my family and friends and apologize sincerely for the pain I am going to cause them," I immediately said, "I forgive you, Patty." From a mother's point of view there is nothing a mother can't forgive her child. Our daughter, Jeanne, told us she had finally forgiven Patty on May 3rd of 2006. It certainly is better to wait until one really means it. When asking Jeanne how she arrived at forgiveness, she said that when they were growing up together, she could eventually forgive her sister anything. It just took her a while because she thought Patty deserted her and now she would be alone when dad and I died. She had always thought she and Patty would have each other's support when we died. She thought the pain, grief, and tasks to accomplish upon our deaths would be shared. It was hard for her to think of doing those things alone.

At the beginning of Patty's note, she wrote: "I'm so sorry to everyone." The "everyone" included God so I dwell on the great gift of God's mercy and forgiveness for Patty and for all of us.

At the morgue we signed papers that Patty's eyes could be donated to someone. As much as Patty wanted to be an organ donor, none of her other vital organs were intact. But she had carried her driver's license in her hand for identification, her donor sticker, and the sticky note about calling her parents. This was ironical because Patty misplaced her driver's license frequently. Yet she had it in her hand when she jumped.

That night when I came home, I still read the paramedic's report. We were told the autopsy would be done first thing the next day. That night was not a night of sleep. I finally drifted off to sleep at four-thirty in the morning for two hours. With so little sleep, it is amazing how well the next day went.

Because Patty's dad had just been released from the hospital at noon the day Patty died (June 22) after emergency surgery on his knee for a MRSA infection, a flesh eating disease, the morning of June 23rd found us preparing for a home visit from a nurse who had to give Bob an antibiotic intravenously for an hour. This was a three week treatment at home which was very difficult after the trauma of Patty's death. It was especially difficult the very first morning since there was so much we needed to talk about but did not want to do it in front of the nurse. While the nurse gave Bob his treatment, I called Columbia St. Mary's to announce Patty's death at work. I also called Fr. Brian at home and asked him to officiate at Patty's funeral. He had been at Good Shepherd for her first communion, at Duplainville Road's Sts. Peter and Paul for her first reconciliation, and had confirmed her there in 1996. Fr. Brian reminded me he was now an Episcopal priest so that might interfere if we wished to have the funeral at our Catholic parish. Since Patty was at Marquette University when we joined St. James, I didn't think it mattered. St. James had also just received a new pastor who started at our parish the day before Patty died. I hated to put him on the spot, requesting that an Episcopal priest officiate in our church, not knowing the new pastor and what his stand on rubric laws and liturgy was.

I didn't have time to hem haw around so I checked with Bob and Jeanne. Both thought it should be Fr. Brian. If we needed that to work with no friction (which we needed no more of at this time), it meant having a funeral parlor service without a mass. I reminded everyone that the people are the Eucharist anyhow so we had all the right ingredients. Fortunately, our church musician was extremely cooperative even though she and our St. James choir were singing at a liturgical music convention at the Midwest Express Center for the weekend involved. So I only asked her to play the piano/organ and have two singers. I copied song sheets. But the choir came to sing, a total surprise to us.

With that settled, Jeanne suggested we have the service at the Schmidt-Bartelt funeral parlor at the Mayfair location. This was geographically easier for Patty's friends around Milwaukee.

In between all these calls, I watered flowers and talked on the phone to Dr. Jensen who had performed Patty's autopsy at the morgue. He assured me Patty died on impact and said he would mail out his report immediately and told us it would take two weeks for the toxicology report that he had ordered. (When that report arrived two weeks later, the two pills I mentioned earlier did show up).

I called one of my sisters to ask her to call all of my family and give them the news as I did not have time. Jeanne took care of calling our friends. Bob and I drove to his dad's house to personally tell him.

Then I called Steve at his parents' house and asked him to meet us at Patty's apartment at eleven in the morning to help pick out clothes and jewelry for the casket and then to go with us to the funeral parlor for all those decisions. Jeanne and her friend, Amy, got to Patty's apartment in Cudahy first. Steve's parents got him there next, and then Bob and I got there. It was drama walking up the sidewalk we had used so frequently two months before to move Patty here from the east side. I had to stare at the grass below her window where I thought she had died. Bob did not want to stop there yet. So we took the elevator up to her apartment. When we entered Patty's apartment, Steve was sitting with his head in his hands. He got up from the sofa very sadly. Jeanne and Amy came out of the bedroom and greeted us. I had to make my way straight to the window. Right in front of the window stood the yellow-black kitchen stool I had let Patty take from home. She had used it to get to the window ledge. I saw how she had moved the decorative candles aside to make room for her step to the ledge. I had to open the window and see the exact spot on the grass. Unfortunately, I did not realize how this bothered Bob and Jeanne who seemed to fear I might do something stupid. But I had to lean out the window a bit to see the spot where Patty's fragile body landed. You could see the outline of the torso of her body. This was because we had had a drought prior to her death and the grass was getting dry and the maintenance man had to power wash the grass where she died because of the blood. (The whole month of July going there to clean out her possessions, I noticed how green the grass grew on that spot: just the way Patty's life is still thriving with God).

Jeanne and Amy found the right clothes for Patty in the casket (had to be high on the neck because of the autopsy). And Steve picked out her jewelry.

Then we took off together to the funeral home to meet with Jim at Schmidt-Bartelt. It was quite an experience even though Bob and I had each done this before. It is quite another thing when you are making choices for your dead daughter. And it was quite traumatic for Jeanne and Steve who had never done this before and who each felt like this was the closest person in the world to them. There was lots of crying and frank conversation. Steve's parents thanked us frequently for letting Steve be an intimate part of this planning and spending the time with us. I was so grateful that he wanted to do it.

By the time we finished we had the hard decisions made, the newspaper article done, flowers ordered, the memorial card, "I'm Free," picked out, and the date finalized to Sunday, June 26, 2005 with the wake from four to seven, followed by the service. Cremation would be the next morning: June 27th.

We then contacted Fr. Brian and Jackie, (a friend of ours who would do the readings at the funeral), to see if they could meet at our house on Friday, the 24th to plan the funeral ceremony. That worked for them and we again included Steve in this planning. Part of the very fruitful conversation we had (besides choosing the readings and writing the petitions) was conversation that we always said we wanted to love each other and not drive each other away because of the pain of Patty's death. So Father encouraged us to actually express that love to each other verbally. Then Bob had a chance to cry and tell how hard it was to tell his own father that Patty was dead. Jeanne had a chance to cry and say: "We were taught in CCD that you are condemned if you die by suicide. I don't want that for my sister." Father gave her very good reassurances that God had forgiven all of us way up front. God's forgiveness is *before* rather than *after* as he knows our nature. Fr. Brian carried that idea out in his funeral homily in the section on "the forgiveness of sin." We all value God's forgiving parental nature and his great mercy. I also reminded Jeanne that Patty had asked God to forgive her, too, in her note. The above discussion made me ask myself many times: how could the church ever have preached such a concept about suicide? As I accept and deal with suicide in our own direct family, I am wondering if suicide is possibly a viable choice for certain people. Personally, I think I'm too selfish for that choice. Or is it possible that suicide is not a choice at all? *Suicide happens* and when it does it is supposed to change the lives of all of us that it touches. I *fight* that my *change* will be for the good of mankind.

After Fr. Brian and Jackie left our house on the 24th, Jeanne and Steve worked on picking out photos to put on picture boards at the funeral home. I worked on two songs for the funeral: David Haas's "You Are Mine" and "With You by My Side." Steve chose the third one: "My Immortal" by Evanescence. During this time Bob stepped out on the patio. The sky was clear; the stars and moon were beautiful. Bob in his mind talked to Patty. He told her it would be really nice if she could send us some rain to end the drought we were having. After Bob was inside about ten minutes I heard it raining and did not pay much attention to it. All at once Bob said, "What's that noise?" I said, "It's just rain." He got very excited and came over to tell me what he had asked of Patty. From then on we referred to her as our "Patty Power." While we were busy with all the funeral details, Patty kept the rain coming every other day so I could quit watering the flowers and take care of settling her matters. The night of the funeral it rained while we drove from the funeral home to Maxim's for dinner, a restaurant where Patty had waitressed. I was very grateful for this rain so that I did not have to water flowers.

On the day of the wake and funeral, a lady at church told me, "You will be amazed at the number of people you will help grieve today." She was correct. On Sunday, June 26, 2005 as Bob drove the van to the funeral home, I sat in the back holding down items for the display so they would not fly around and get wrecked. I really got sick to my stomach back there. When I got to the funeral home, the funeral director was very nervous talking to me before we viewed Patty the first time. When I entered the room where Patty was, at a distance she looked like she was sleeping on the couch or her old maple twin bed. When I arrived at the coffin, I looked over her body and started to feel so bad at the large wide bruise on the middle of her forehead, the freckles on her nose that had turned black, her swollen neck, swollen arms, and dark finger nails. In my mind I started to question whether it had been a good decision to show Patty. But in an instant, I got an answer which was: *it will be good for her young friends to stare death in the face. Death is a reality that we cannot wish away. After all, the minute we are born, the count-down to our death begins. This funeral of Patty must testify to that truth.*

Then I wanted to touch Patty but I did not want to kiss her face because I wanted forever to remember what Patty felt like whenever I hugged and kissed her very soft, warm body with vibrant life in it. So instead I grasped both her arms and tried to cradle them in my embrace. When I did that, a very strong sense of peace and calm flowed through me from head to toe. It was as if someone had thrown a blanket of peace over me. I had no more stomach butterflies or sickness. Instead I felt immense happiness for Patty. I know it was Patty letting me know she was all right and that I need not worry about her anymore. It was a transformation moment that prepared me for the wake from four to seven with the funeral to follow.

Two people came early to the funeral home. One was a nurse supervisor of Patty's who spoke very kindly of her and told us Patty was a good nurse. Lynn, a good friend of Patty's also arrived with a thirty by forty inch poster board collage of photos that friends had e-mailed to her. There were many different venues of Patty enjoying her friends whom she valued very much. The heading on the board was: "Patty, we love you!" I still have this collage and treasure it.

During the wake, a science teacher I used to teach with before retirement gave us a small piece of paper on which it said: "No trial has come to you but what is common to everyone. God is faithful and will not let you be tried beyond your strength; but with the trial he will also provide a way out, so that you may be able to bear it." He said someone had given it to him at his wife's funeral and it had helped him a great deal in his grief. He hoped it would do the same for us. Indeed it did. Later I found the text in 1 Corinthians 10:13.

Just before the end of the wake, a friend of Patty's was hugging Steve and sobbing very loud. It was piercing and silenced everyone in the funeral home. The funeral director used the moment to get everyone to be seated and prepare for the service. Fr. Brian had a marvelous homily based on the last four parts of the Apostles Creed. He had submitted it to us before the funeral so that nothing would startle us.

Father Brian's Funeral Homily delivered on June 26, 2005

When Patty's mom phoned me Thursday morning, I – like the rest of us – was shocked to hear the terrible news. And when I visited with Patty's parents – Lois and Bob, Patty's sister Jeanne, and Patty's dear boy friend Steve Friday afternoon – I left with no idea what words could possibly speak to their grief and to our grief. So yesterday I went to the scene itself in Cudahy, to think, to pray, and to ask Patty what could possibly speak to the terrible sorrow everyone feels. There on the lawn, I found a single purple rose someone – perhaps one of you – left, with a note attached reading: *"Beautiful Girl, may you rest in peace."* I prayed those words, *"Beautiful Girl, may you rest in peace"* over and over. As I prayed, the last four articles of the "Apostles Creed" came to me with a clarity I've never before known: **"We believe in the communion of saints, the forgiveness of sins, the resurrection of the body, and life everlasting."** This is what I think Patty would say to our grief.

So, FIRST: "We believe in the <u>Communion of Saints</u>"

- Now this word "saints" isn't meant to imply the apostles or martyrs, or some ceramic or concrete image of a holy person we'd find in a church or in a garden. The word "saint" refers to the Baptized, those who believe in Jesus, those washed in the waters of Baptism.

- Patty. Little Patty. She was two when I was assigned to her home parish. I gave her First Communion, celebrated her First Reconciliation with her, confirmed her, and knew her through the church.

- Patty. Little Patty. Her bunnies (some forty over the years) . . . voracious reader . . . 4 – H . . . the county fairs . . . ribbons, trophies, and medals . . . high school . . . volleyball . . . basketball . . . her letter jacket . . . waitressing . . . cutting wedding cakes for hours on end on Saturdays . . . Marquette . . . graduation . . . UW-MIL . . . therapist . . . nurse . . . friend . . . friendly. Jeanne, being three years older, may have made it easier for Patty to learn to drive and date, but Patty's being a perfectionist and a worrier with a need to succeed, unable to function any longer is a cross Patty carried all by herself.

- We are all members of the Communion of Saints. Baptism unites us to Jesus and to one another with bonds that cannot be broken. And Patty is and will always be a treasured member of the Communion of Saints.

SECOND: "We believe in the <u>Forgiveness of Sins</u>"

- A word we hate to say is "suicide" – and when we do we do so in hushed tones. Two other words we hate to acknowledge: "depression" and "despair." Because we try not to notice depression and despair in our daily lives we're forced to say the word suicide today.

- Patty was up against too much. Who knew? Who to talk to? Fear of failure . . . fear of not measuring up to her own high standards . . . pressured to the breaking point . . . easier to ask forgiveness for taking her life than to ask forgiveness for possibly failing at work.

- Do we forgive Patty? Of course. And do we forgive ourselves? We need to, but not too quickly. We need to learn from this tragedy, and maybe it means for us to risk caring and loving and listening to one another better than we have up until now.

- Does God forgive Patty? Why would God not? How could

God not? God is the Giver of life, the Author of love, and the Inventor of forgiveness.

- We so misunderstand the word "forgiveness." It means to "give" what's needed "before" it's even needed or requested.

- We incorrectly use the word "forgiveness" when we actually mean and practice "aftergiveness." Someone says or does something and asks our forgiveness, and "after" the fact we reluctantly "give" it with strings attached . . . but that person had better never do or say it again . . . or else!

- But God invented the gift of forgiveness, and forgave us 2000 years ago in the death of Jesus on the cross. Jesus forgave Patty and us then and there. There isn't anything we can do to deserve that forgiveness. It's a gift from God. God forgives as only God can. And we can't limit the goodness of God!

THIRD: "We believe in the <u>Resurrection of the Body</u>"

- In Mark's gospel, there's the raising of the daughter of Jairus. A little girl, age 12, lies dead. Jesus bent over her, took her by the hand, and lovingly said to her: *"Little girl, get up!"* And she did. And that's what Jesus did on Wednesday when Patty lay dead. He bent over her, took her by the hand, and lovingly said to her: *"Little girl, get up"* from your former life. Come home with Me, be safe, and be at peace with Me in heaven.

- In Matthew's gospel, Jesus said, when you're burdened or overwhelmed, when your burdens are entirely too much for you to carry alone: "Come to Me."

- In John's gospel, at the Last Supper, Jesus promised that in heaven there are many dwelling places, one for each of us. He said He would have to go ahead of us (His death), but that He would come back (His resurrection), and having prepared our place for us, He would take us with Him (our death), so that where He is we also may be. Now, I grant you, we weigh promises on the credibility and trustworthiness of the one making the promise. But Jesus is our Savior, and He makes good on His promises.

- St. Paul, in one of his letters, asked what could possibly ever separate us from the love of God. He lists all sorts of disastrous things including life and death – to which we can add depression and despair . . . and Paul concludes that nothing, absolutely nothing, could ever separate us from the love of God.

- On Wednesday, Patty fell into the safe arms of her Savior and her Good Shepherd, Who in Matthew's gospel promised to remember: *"You came to visit Me when I was sick"* . . . *as a therapist . . . as a nurse . . . as a friend. "Whatever you did for one of my least sisters or brothers, you did it for Me! Come! Enter into the joy of heaven!"*

FOURTH: "We believe in <u>Life Everlasting</u>"

- I was so glad on Friday when Patty's family reminded me that "eternal life" doesn't begin when we pass from this life, but it begins at our Baptism.

- Patty, a member of the *Communion of Saints*, promised the *Forgiveness of Sins* and the *Resurrection of the Body* already began *Life Everlasting* twenty-six years ago.

- Patty unquestionably lived an incredibly good life – a loving, caring, giving, gentle life . . . and is now with God.

- But we – as difficult and as heart-breaking as it is – we must bid a tearful but faith-and-hope-filled farewell . . . until one day the God of love reunites us all.

- Yes, *"Beautiful Girl, may you rest in peace."* Amen.

After Fr. Brian's delivery, he asked people to express anything about Patty that they wished. I started by simply saying: "Love." That is what Patty was to me. Patty's greatest tribute was then given by a fellow nurse who said Patty was a good nurse and that no patient was "too little" or "too least" for Patty, from grumpy old men to dementia patients. Patty treated them all compassionately. This tribute echoes Matthew 25:34 - 40 when Jesus said, "Whatever you did for one of the least of these brothers of mine, you did for me." This comment touched me greatly. It assured me I need not worry about Patty's happiness with God. I knew she was all right.

My sister, Kathy, offered this prayer to be included at the end of our prayer service: "May Patty's life be an inspiration to all of us in her compassion and kindness for the people she cared for in her work, and with her friends and family."

The day after the funeral, I drove to the funeral home to get the photo boards and flowers. When I transported the two huge bouquets of roses, five broken roses cracked off in the van. After unloading everything, there were the five scattered roses, desolate looking in the flatbed of the van. They reminded me of Bob, Jeanne, Patty, me, and Steve. We were all broken, cracked off, and desolate. The next day in a Care Note I read this quote from Karen Katafiasz: *"Be open to the pain of your broken heart. God enters through its brokenness."*

It also dawned on me that the month Patty died was our thirty-third wedding anniversary. If I was into Biblical numbers, I'd remember that some scholars think Christ died and rose at age thirty-three. If I made an analogy to His life, I would realize this traumatic experience of losing Patty was our Calvary and somehow we would have to rise above it. The rising would take work and God's help. Maybe my going public on suicide would be my public ministry.

Exactly one week after Patty's transition, we went to her apartment to check on bills and find anything else of importance to help us decide on how to empty the apartment. After about a half hour there going through Patty's bills, I started to get sick to my stomach. As I began to think about leaving, Bob came into the office I was working in and said: "Let's go now." I agreed, looked at my watch, and noted it was five in the afternoon. I could not help but note that it was exactly one week ago at this time of day that Patty had jumped out the window. If only we had been here a week ago. No wonder we felt sick. As we got in the car and drove away, I asked Bob: "How are we going to get through this if we can't stand being here?" He said we should plan carefully what we could bring home each day. At first get the biggest items so the van and trailer get filled quickly, keeping our time there to a minimum. That worked. As we progressed through the month of July, I grew fond of going to her place. On the very last day as I locked the door to leave, I felt sad that I would not be back to her final place of residence.

During the clean-out time, I brought home some laundry Patty had in the living room. She must have been planning to do it the day she died. As I sorted the clothing for the laundry, I picked off long strands of Patty's strawberry blonde hair and reverently saved it in a baggy. It made me think of when she was growing up at home. I usually had to pick her long strands of hair off her bed sheets and clothing before laundering them because her hair was so fine and full of static. I always knew I would treasure those laundry moments. It made me think that we must take time to enjoy the *little* things in life because someday we will look back and realize they were the *big* ones.

Another frustration we experienced was: what could we do with the beautiful sectional sofa set Patty had delivered just two weeks before she died? I really did not want to keep it. I felt better about returning it to the store since it was only two weeks old and had all the tags on the pieces yet. However, because it was a custom order (taupe color), the store wanted a six hundred dollar re-shelving fee if it was returned. I did not want to pay that fee so we kept the sectional for our house. As frustrating as the whole experience was, I marveled that Patty had chosen a color I would have chosen. On top of that, it fit beautifully in our new great room. We did learn to enjoy its use and by Thanksgiving time cut off the tags, agreeing we would keep the set.

During the first few days of July I had felt a strong awareness of Patty's presence with me. When I got out of bed at seven-twenty in the morning on July 6, 2005, to go to the bathroom, my mind was an absolute blank. I was still groggy from sleep. My mind got the message: "I'm okay, Mom. I have no pain." It happened so fast that I sat on the side of the bed and asked myself: *"What was that?"* I totally forgot about going to the bathroom and had to tell my husband what had happened. It was an experience that brought great solace to me.

In August I again had several weeks of feeling a strong presence of Patty. It almost started to sadden me because I wondered if what I felt was normal. It was then that I struggled with my inside feeling of not really wanting Patty's death to be a reality. Then I finally thought through the idea that it would be so wrong to even wish Patty back here in this awful life compared to the hereafter. How could I morally even consider asking her to re-enter the mind torture she endured here? Here is when I tried harder to have compassion for what Patty was living with in her mind. I began to understand better the way Patty perceived her life, very differently than the way we perceived her life. She did not experience the same confidence in her life that we thought she should have because of how capable she was. I believe she suffered much more in this life than we will ever know. I also believe that now she sees things as they really are and realizes that things could have been worked out and problems could have been solved with communication and support from us and professionals. But she has won the lottery or gone on vacation or graduated to that next stage of life and is happier for it. So it is simply up to us to handle our grief and pain and get on with life. I do believe Patty can help us do that by helping us understand that she is okay in her Spirit life. I believe her mission in her transformed life is to minister to us by helping us achieve peace. She brings us peace by making our minds and hearts at home with who we are and how we are.

In the reading I have done of other suicide victims, half of the survivors' grief seemed to exist around not knowing why their loved one was a victim of suicide. Less than one fourth of suicide victims leave a note. We were so fortunate to have Patty's note. Though the reading of her note still gravely effects me, I am so grateful that Patty wrote it to all of us (see Chapter 7).

It was after this kind of thinking developed in me, that I could finally get back to a more personal relationship with God. I never felt angry with God over the situation and don't know if I ever will. I do know I felt a bit numb, but always knew God was there for me, though I could not understand what was happening. But that's life, always a bit of mystery to it. The author of *A Grief Unveiled* says: "Suffering is the heat that softens our hearts." He also maintains that in grief there is a mathematical equation that pain/grief/suffering equals intensity of love. I do strongly agree with this idea. I am proud of my pain because I know that I loved and continue to love Patty. My relationship with her is "forever" and that gives me great consolation.

Another story I love to remember was an example Jacquelyn Oliveira gave in one of her talks. She spoke of a man who found a cocoon in his garden. It was just starting to open. So he helped and finished opening it and then placed the caterpillar-butterfly in a protective container. About three days later it died. The scientific knowledge then given this gardener was that he should have let nature run its course. The strength it would have taken the caterpillar to very gradually open his cocoon himself was the very development he needed in his body later to survive. She then compared this to humans working through the painful process of grief. Once we have a significant loss, the grief work develops strengths in us that we need to survive or we will always be in a cocoon that imprisons us.

My third experience with Patty's Spirit happened November 7, 2005 and really shocked me to the point of giving me a headache for four days. I attempt to meditate and read Scripture while I exercise on a bicycle when I first get up in the morning. This particular morning I was dreading the fact that I would see a great number of relatives this day from my hometown: relatives who had not been to Patty's funeral and ones who had very traditional Catholic outlooks on suicide. As I moved into my God connection with Scripture, a huge wave of grief overcame me and I sobbed heavily and said to God in my mind, *"After all these months since June 22nd, I have been telling you I accept this reality because I have to. It really happened. But I don't want to accept it any more. I was kidding myself. I really don't want to accept this death. I really want*

Patty to be here again physically." Right in the middle of this burst of grief, Patty interrupts me and says in my mind, "But mom, you know how much I hurt in my head and how much pain it caused me even in my body. Remember my back pain and how miserable I was." I had a visual of Patty's head in my mind on the right side. Because I had been so emotional when this happened, I felt stunned, shocked. I did not even tell my husband until four days had passed and I could not stand the headache any longer. When I related the story to my husband, Bob, he suggested I go to the chiropractor as the situation's stress probably settled in my neck area and upper shoulders. He was correct. One visit and the stress was relieved and no more headache. I did have to ask Patty to back off a bit. This last experience was too dramatic for me. Now I try to be aware of her touch in the ordinary yet wonderful touches she adds to our lives.

An opportunity presented itself for me to express these experiences to a psychologist I used to work with when I was teaching. He had now become a minister in our community. After telling him these events, he responded that he did believe in such spiritual connections. He narrated a couple such experiences he had had with parishioner's deceased family members. He thought perhaps Patty wanted to comply with my request I made to her the evening I was waiting for the police to come to our house. He also said that Patty's note indicated apology for the pain her death would cause us so that her Spirit, no doubt, wanted to comfort me and assure me she was okay and I need not worry about her. Since I was "getting" her message and seemed to be satisfied Patty was all right in her Spirit world, she had no need to continue.

Another professional scientist who totally supports these experiences with the Spirit world is Elizabeth Kubler-Ross, MD. In her book titled, *On Life after Death,* she relates observations and experiences of more than twenty thousand dying and near-death experiences all over the world. After her own documentation of such phenomenon, she says one should not worry about convincing skeptics who give you a hard time about life after death. She humorously says they will find out the truth when they die.

I love Patty eternally and am so grateful that she loves me enough to make me feel her presence. Sometimes I can momentarily overcome the grief by the happiness of knowing Patty's Spirit is right here with me. Patty's presence makes resurrection a reality for me. I bought a silver bracelet engraved with the words: "I am always with you...." This is my reminder from Scripture that God and Patty are always with me. This comforts me a great deal. I also started a collection of Scripture passages that use those words.

One night I had a dream while we were in Hershey, Pennsylvania. It was November 6, 2006. In the dream I was with Patty (assumed I was in eternity with her). I was so overjoyed and happy to see her again and be with her. I was so excited. Her presence was a real happiness trigger. Her appearance was more youthful than an adult but different and more mature than her elementary-school face. Her hair was more imaginary but a blonde version somewhat shorter than she usually wore it. She wore the color pink. Even though I thought I held her, hugged her, and kissed her, I can't tell you what she felt like. Her presence was the exhilarator, an assurance that she would always be with me. She made me so happy. My overall secure feeling was that I had made it to the other side of life with her. Then my female principal from St. Mary's, Hales Corners came along. She asked me if she could let me and my student into my locked classroom. As I looked up, I saw the seventh-grade classroom door with the glass side-light of the room I had taught in at St. Mary's in the 1960's. I was surprised that the principal could also see Patty because I thought Patty and I would be invisible to those on earth. I declined the principal's offer to unlock my classroom door, told her I had my own key, unlocked the door, and walked into the classroom. Once inside the classroom, I was alone. I was disappointed that the principal had interrupted my time with Patty. The dream ended and I noted the time was three-forty in the morning.

I was overjoyed with my dream of Patty. It was a "joy" I'd been asking of her when my mind would plea: *"Give me joy again, Patty, to overcome some of the pain."*

On November 16, 2006 when I called my sister, Doris, she told me my principal had died at Campbellsport. I asked Doris to look up the date she had died. After checking the death notice, Doris confirmed that the death date was November 6th. So I guess my principal was the lucky one. She was the one in eternity with Patty, not me. No wonder I ended up alone in the classroom at the end of the dream. The dream must have been the principal's treat for me as I had sent her a heartfelt farewell letter just before she moved to Campbellsport with terminal cancer.

I feel like St. Paul when he said he lived with one foot in this world and one foot in the next, living between the *old* age and the *new* age. I was so into this spirit world of Patty's that on June 15, 2006 (one week before the first anniversary of Patty's death), I thought I was having a heart attack when I had severe chest pains. I decided *not* to call 911, went to lie down on the bed, closed my eyes, and decided to just let the pain take its course. The pain got worse. In my mind I thought: *God and Patty, I'm ready for this transition. I'll be with Patty again.* I was ready to die. I had no fear. Then I just let my mind drift in peace. All of a sudden I realized that the next day was Jeanne's birthday. She already hated her birthday because last year her birthday was the last day she saw Patty alive. Now if I died the day before celebrating her birthday, it would be the second family death so close to her birthday. I could not do that. So I made a conscious decision to live, as Deuteronomy says: "Choose Life!" So I carefully got out of bed with new energy, went slowly to the kitchen by hanging on to things, ate a small portion of apple sauce, and gradually got rid of the pain. I have often wondered what this attack was. Was it indigestion which I had never experienced before? I don't know. I do know that the incident renewed my motivation to make sure Patty's death never overshadowed the lives of my loved ones present to me now in physical form. And the experience was an important decision in my healing.

Sometimes I think Patty's death was like receiving a bullet shot between my eyes. It was that sudden, out of the ordinary, that shocking, that mind numbing, that paralyzing, that difficult to recover from, and that sensitive to the human mind because the bullet cannot be removed. It will forever affect me, sometimes be more painful, create in me emotions and thoughts I never knew existed, and instill in me compassion and understanding. Part of the mourning and grief involves discovering a new *identity* individually and as a family, an identity that still relates to Patty on her side of life.

We recognize our brokenness. Brokenness is not to be feared.
It is to be embraced to strengthen us. Then it cannot destroy us.

CHAPTER 2

How I Survive

"Lord, help me to remember that nothing is going
to happen to me today that
You and I together can't handle."
An old preacher's greeting to each new day

Some of the following ways of expressing my grief are very personal. They are not meaningful to everyone. They are only meant as examples or possibilities of how you can express yourself at such a sad time. Naturally each griever will discern his/her own avenue of expression. I do think it is important for you to find some tangible way to comfort and console yourself.

- The night Patty died I asked her to let me know every day of my life that she is okay and happy. She does that. Every day I try to be aware of when she touches my life. Some days it is very evident and remarkable. There are some amazing times when my husband and I see a young gal who resembles Patty. This gives us great joy!

- Immediately I made two memory binders of Patty including funeral items, some special mementoes and poetry written by a boy friend, special photos used at her funeral, special cards she wrote to us over the years, special e-mail messages written to us after her death by her friends on the Journal's website, a special tribute by an aunt and a friend out of town who could not come to the funeral, and letters her sister and I mailed to each other the first few months after her death.

- In addition Jeanne organized some special photos of Patty and friends and had her boy friend arrange them to special music on a DVD. Playing that DVD frequently was very healing as well as looking at all the above albums.

- Within the first month, I gave myself space between canceling Patty's credit cards, returning brand new merchandize with receipts, stopping utility services, and cleaning out her apartment. In between these very sad tasks, I read every sympathy card with its verses and every letter friends and family sent us. Each day I spent some time writing back to these correspondents expressing gratitude for thinking of us and for lifting us up in prayer. I am convinced it was their prayers that gave us the strength to endure and live again.

- We gave the memorial donations people gave us to the Columbia St. Mary Foundation because Patty was a nurse at Columbia St. Mary's. We continued to give to this foundation for about five years and then decided to place Patty's name on our own Charitable Giving Fund.

- We had a special ceramic urn made for Patty's ashes and keep it in a prominent place in our home. A few of her ashes were given to her sister, Jeanne. We also scattered a few of her ashes on two volleyball courts where Patty and her friends play.

- Every day I tell Patty I love her. The love bond between us is forever.

- Constant reading on suicide and loss of a child helped me, especially the first year. I read as many suicide accounts as

I could from books, magazines, and workshop handouts. It helped me to see that suicide is a common cause of death. It proved that we were not alone in this "suicide soup." People at church and in the neighborhood came out of the woodwork and shared the suicide experience in their families.

- Morning and evening prayers are important to me. I pray for those who will be suicide victims today and their families. Prayer after Patty's death has taken on a new meaning for me. I rest in God now hoping to see His side of this event, His love of Patty, and ask to grow in acceptance.

- Daily meditation and spiritual reading on the Scripture readings of the day are important to me. Realizing prayer is real energy and that Patty is now energy, prayer has become an experience of communion with God and Patty. As Mary Marrocco says, prayer is "air to breath and water to drink."

- Morning exercise accompanies the meditation as often as possible. The physical movement seems to stimulate my meditation. Both of these activities are important to the griever's physical and mental health.

- In my night prayers I ask Patty to help her sister, her sister's boy friend, Patty's Steve, and other special friends and relatives. She has responded remarkably. For this I am so grateful. As some say: "Energy flows to where attention goes." God is Divine Energy. Prayer is a kind of energy and so is the form of life Patty lives in now.

- Every night when I go to bed I sleep peacefully remembering God's and Patty's presence in my heart. I always ask her Spirit to be with me. The first year I had to place both my hands over my heart to feel the beats pulsing and say over and over the mantra: "God and Patty." Somehow feeling life beat within me put me in touch with God's life and the life Patty still lives.

- Frequently I can feel the energy of Patty's presence. I know she is still with me. I just can't see her. I bought a sterling silver bracelet on which was engraved: "I am always with you…" My favorite Scripture verse is: "Do not be afraid. I am always with you." I have kept a list of locations in the Bible where this appears.

  In 2011 I gave this bracelet to my sister, Sr. Anne, when she was dying in hospice. She began to cry so I said the verse: "Do not be afraid. I am always with you." Anne had the bracelet on when she died. She was Patty's god-mother. She died at the same time of day as Patty did. This fact really consoled me. It made me feel Patty was present for Anne's transition from this life.

- About two months after Patty died, I drove around the city and photographed the places Patty worked and lived: all high school and college jobs, dorms at Marquette, apartments, and her hospital job at the time of her death. The trip was full of memories, remembering meeting her at these various places throughout the years.

- On her first birthday after her death we gave a party for her many friends (as that was a practice she had with her friends). At the party we gave out picture cards of Patty with her birth date and in place of a death date, I wrote: "Patty now lives life in a form we cannot see." On the back side we printed her compassionate philosophy of life.

- On Patty's birthday and anniversary of her death, my husband and I visit the spot where Patty made her transition to the next stage of life (a sacred place). Once in a while we also stop over to watch her friends play volleyball on the south side. As we approached the seventh anniversary of

Patty's transition, my husband asked me if it was necessary to always go to the spot of Patty's death. I responded that he did not have to go this year if he did not want to, but I was going to go because I think it is a sacred place because that is where Patty became a Spirit. He did go with me as usual. After we walk slowly passed her spot, we sit on a park bench in silence to pray and meditate, staring at Lake Michigan. Sometimes we say a prayer out loud.

• I worked on the attitude: better to have had twenty-six years of the gift of Patty than not to have had her at all. I really mean this because I think of the love I have for Patty that would be totally missing in my life if we had not had a second child.

• Another attitude I developed was to love those who are still physically present. I reminded family "it is not about us but about Patty." I tried to be more mindful of Patty's suffering before her death rather than my suffering.

• I remind myself constantly that everyone in the world has a suffering. Not having Patty physically present just happens to be mine. Others are also experiencing a death in the family, cancer, chronic illness, divorce, desertion, abuse (physical, verbal, or emotional), mental illness, relationship struggles, loss of jobs, problem children, or alcoholism, etc. So why should I be an exception to the rule that everyone in this life suffers? Why shouldn't I be like everyone else? So instead of asking "Why," the question should be: "Why not?"

• I asked Jeanne to call us daily for a time for all of our sakes. We also met her once a week for lunch or dinner. After six months, the phone calls were further apart; and after two years, our eating out together became less frequent.

• The first year I frequently played the CD's of the songs we used for Patty's funeral. One song about God being by my side was especially strengthening. Another very inspirational song was on the Celtic Woman CD: "You Raise Me Up."

- I had many one on one lunches at my home with friends from church and bible study. It was a very comfortable setting to really talk and get into ideas. All this chatting was very good for me, getting everything out in the open.

- Friends and family were very helpful: my youngest sister and husband who had experienced loss, Vagabond Ski Club friends who had similar losses of children, and occasionally meeting bereaved parents at church functions or workshops to share stories.

- About ten months after Patty died I spoke to the married couple who found Patty on the ground after she jumped. It helped me very much because I was feeling cheated that I was not present for her death, considering I did give birth to her. I'm sure God knows best. I do not have the control. God does. But I can control *how I respond, remembering* He is the Creator and I am the creature.

  After speaking with this married couple on Holy Saturday, I had a much better Easter Sunday. When I showered, I would imagine Patty jumping out the window of her apartment and try to experience her last moments. Having the couple answer my questions and give descriptions of what I wanted to know helped eliminate these images and mental visualizations I used to get in my mind.

- Special gifts had meaning and significance. My youngest sister gave us a framed poem, "Letter from Heaven." She also made a quilt out of scanned photos of significant events in Patty's life on pieces of Patty's clothing. She surprised us with it the second Christmas after Patty's transformation. Another sister at our first Thanksgiving brought a special tall glass candle with names of our family's deceased members on it, including Patty's. Two other sisters gave us a meaningful framed poem based on a Native American prayer. Another sister gave me a pillow the first Christmas that had these words stitched into it: "If you know that God's hand is in everything, you can leave everything in God's hand."

- For Jeanne's birthday gift, I had a portrait painted of Jeanne and Patty. Jeanne had seen Patty the last time on Jeanne's birthday.

- The first few Christmases I made an effort to look through our family photo albums. Gradually we have changed our celebration of Thanksgiving and Christmas. Making it different from our traditions prior to Patty's death does help.

- Because I believe in the Hebrew word for angel that means "messenger of God," (with many people in our lives serving that mission) and also because Patty had quite an angel collection from high school, I devoted the top portion of our Christmas tree to special angels I found when traveling after her death. "Patty, you were a messenger of God in our lives and we didn't know it until June 22, 2005."

- Frequently I wear some of Patty's jewelry. Even though we had to vacate her apartment and distribute her possessions in about a three week period, my husband and I kept some very meaningful possessions of hers that we treasure just because they belonged to Patty, including two full journals she had written. Special pictures she had drawn and ceramics she made are wonderful to have and admire. We also gave some special things to her sister who was very hesitant to pick anything out even though we invited her to do so. We also gave some of Patty's jewelry to her friends.

- I bring up Patty's name on a regular basis with family and friends. I don't want to hide the precious gift she was.

- I have nurtured two special house plants from Patty's funeral. As they grow by leaps and bounds, I'm reminded of her blooming on her side of life. After five years, I gave the largest plant to a good friend. I separated with the last English ivy plant after the seventh anniversary. I think I am healing.

- I talk very openly about death and suicide. As a result, people (sometimes complete strangers) tell me some amazing stories about themselves. Families disclose their suicide stories. A woman, twenty-five, told me about her three attempts at suicide and how she got well. She was now married, had a child, and was getting her degree in college.

"The only feelings that do not heal are the ones you hide."
Henri Nouwen

- Journaling was a tremendous outlet. I used two started journals I found in Patty's apartment. I used the black one with yellow smiley faces to write my emotional reactions after her death. Some entries were letters I wrote to Patty. Some entries described beautiful dreams I had of Patty. Dreaming about her is wonderful. I used a second journal of hers to write inspirational ideas that I would read in books or Care Notes or pamphlets.

I bought one brand new journal to write special Scripture verses that struck me as bearing thought on Patty's death or our grief, including ones that gave meaning to our hope and faith in resurrection. I do believe our loved ones experience resurrection immediately as Jesus did.

See Chapter 9 for a list of some of the Scripture passages I used to meditate on that were very touching in my healing process. Every one of them said something special to me about Patty or her transition or our trauma afterwards. Sometimes the passages were instructive on how to deal with suffering.

- Word of God study: I stayed involved in Metro Bible Study as one of the facilitators to lead weekly discussions on our study of the year (an annual study from September through March).

  In my study of the Word of God, I accumulated lists of references on certain themes such as "God is Faithful," verses using the words tears, mourn, grieve, or "Do not be afraid." Suggestion: you should start your own list. It is more meaningful when it is based on personal preference.

- Grief seminars such as Jacquelyn Oliveira's were and are very helpful, especially the one on "Healing through Grief." They help us see that grieving must be accomplished and is very different for each individual.

- I collect Fr. Ron Rolheiser's articles on suicide from the Catholic Herald. He writes one every year. They are excellent articles. I would recommend these articles to anyone, no matter what religious affiliation one has. These articles on suicide are now on his website @ www.ronrolheiser.com. I was able to go back as far as 1985 on this topic.

- I made a list of good coming out of Patty's death. See Chapter 10.

- We continued to travel as had been our practice after retirement. Patty's Spirit goes with us. We feel Patty help us on these trips to rekindle our own love for each other and with safety of travel.

- We celebrate her name's day, March 17th, St. Patty's Day.

- Gardening, especially flowers, served as great therapy and naturally provided many analogies to real life. I wrote a chapter on the learning I gleaned. See Chapter 11. In my flower gardens I have collected some neat plaques with quotations about a loved one we miss and some great statues that remind us of Patty and her sister, Jeanne.

- I continued my work with our bereavement ministry at my parish. It also naturally increased with friends outside my parish as I became more comfortable speaking about death and wanting to reach out to others suffering grief.

- I stayed involved with our sister parish in the inner city where we were working together on a rehab house. Bob and I picked up donated furniture and appliances from donors in our community and delivered them to homes in need in the inner city.

- We became active in our parish St. Vincent de Paul Conference in 2006. We go on home visits to hear the stories and needs of those we serve. We attempt to help them problem solve and put them in touch with resources. After careful discernment, many times we are able to give some financial assistance. We find it especially touching when a client is a young woman with children. Some clients suffer from panic attacks. Many times on these home visits our experience of being touched by these families gives us a distinct feeling Patty is sending them into our lives. We know we benefit by helping in this way, something we can no longer do for Patty.

- I believe it is now Patty's mission in the stage of life she enjoys to minister to me, my husband, and her sister, Jeanne, and to her own many friends. We are happy to say that Patty is doing her job. We call her our "Patty Power."

- In trying to understand Patty's transformation into the next stage of life, I make an attempt to prepare myself for my transformation, to be ready at all times for we know not the hour. That applies not only to the end of my physical life but to my present living, trying to be aware of what God is revealing to me in my life every day.

• Images of butterflies are important to me because of the transformation they experience. There is a neat story about caterpillars wondering what happened to fellow caterpillars because they disappeared after climbing to the top of the flower stems. One day they too climbed to the top of the stem, transformed into butterflies, and flew away.

• John Shea's three books on the Sunday Gospels have been great meditation sources for me. My favorite sections were on spiritual presence and resurrection. The main title is: *The Spiritual Wisdom of the Gospels for Christian Preachers and Teachers, Year A, Year B, Year C.* Each year is a separate book.

Having studied a great deal of science in my life, I also appreciated John Shea's treatment of grievers who related their scientific knowledge to their spirituality. Some of our science laws actually help us grasp some of the Spirit world.

• These movies were very helpful and meaningful: *Ordinary People, After Jimmy, Hereafter, Unsaid, and The Greatest.*"

• We have accepted that we are not in control. We learned this in 1980 when Patty almost died in the seizure. The same year my sister, Sister Cecelia died. Then during spring break we lost Jeanne, our oldest daughter, in Florida. It was very scary as we searched for Jeanne about twenty minutes at the resort. It was the same time "Adam" had been kidnapped in the national news. While we were scouring the resort, I had visions of someone kidnapping her and flying off to California. Eventually, a young father came to the front desk holding Jeanne's hand. He had found her in the parking lot;

she had tried to catch up to her dad going to the store. We were so fortunate that no one backed a car over her as she was very short, being less than four years old. Experience is the best teacher to convince us that we do not have control over events. We can only choose to respond to the events with God's mind-set. We must now apply this principle to Patty's transformation on June 22, 2005.

> *"He who conceals his grief*
> *Finds no remedy for it."*
> *Turkish Proverb*

CHAPTER 3

Verbalizing our Grief

"The only feelings that do not heal are the ones you hide."
Henri Nouwen

There is no doubt in my mind that God helped us in a marvelous way after Patty's death. His power and guidance led us to sources of knowledge and inspiration. His Spirit inspired us in these letters and writings. Even now when I doubt and question, I have to reread the following letters to bolster my faith and understanding.

This letter arrived a few weeks after Patty died.

You know it has taken me weeks to figure out how to start this letter, mostly because I never thought that I would be writing something like this. This is a letter twenty-six years overdue. So here it goes:

Dear Mom and Dad,

I thank you for the greatest gift ever given to me. Thank you for Patty. She was unique. She was the most fun to know. No one has ever ticked me off more, but I could never stay mad at her. The mere sight of her comforts me more than anything or anyone else in my life - my constant companion over the years. I have had the great pleasure that few others ever experience, my little sister has truly become my *very best friend.* Many people treasure their siblings, but few are as close as Patty and I were. She was my one of a kind. Over the years there have been a number of boy-friends, many different friends, many co-workers, classmates, teammates, multiple relatives, two *wonderful* parents, but I was given only one Patty. Now that she is gone, I truly feel how irreplaceable she is in a way that I did not understand until now. So thank you for twenty-six years with my best friend.

She has brought me more happiness than anyone I have ever known. Unfortunately I now realize this because I am now feeling the most profound sadness my life has ever known. What can I say? She has affected me. She has made me feel emotion. She has touched so many people and will forever be:

Party Patty
–the wild, free spirit
– the compassionate caregiver
–the excellent student
–the gentle little girl
–the great friend who was a wonderful listener
–an outstanding athlete
–the breath of fresh air
–the beautiful girl
–the constant perfectionist

who was perfect, but didn't know it. So even though I will miss her every day for the rest of my life, I will also thank God for every day I had with her.

Thank you!
Love,
Jeanne

The following is my response to Jeanne's letter.

July 22, 2005

Dear Jeanne,

So sorry this letter is late in response to yours which we received on July 21st. I wrote this the day after but left it on scrap paper way too long.

Don't forget God made you and Patty the greatest blessings of my life and dad's. Because of love connecting us, Patty's death leads to great heartache and pain. Yet out of this suffering our love keeps growing between her and us. And in our tremendous grief we should be able to lean on each other and grow in our love for each other and other people in our lives, too.

Our consolation (due to our belief in resurrection), should be that Patty's absence is only temporary. Think of it as Patty being on a long vacation. When we die, we'll be on vacation with her.

Perhaps God's purpose in Patty's life was to have her touch so many lives by her friendliness and compassion so that her death would get everyone's attention, wake us up, make us see what life is really all about. We better be people of faith, people of integrity, authentic people, genuine and without pretension, caring, loving, and compassionate people, convinced we can make a difference in the world.

So we must not stop living because of her death but live better because of her life and how it touched us.

Yes, I thank God daily that He gave me the gift of Patty for twenty-six years of happiness and love. Knowing how great God's love is, I can't fight with Him about His wanting Patty back for Himself. Besides, God probably needed a party organizer in His mystery state called heaven. Knowing how much I (a human), love Patty and always forgave her for anything, I cannot ever doubt God's love and forgiveness for her, especially when she asked for forgiveness in her last letter.

Having witnessed one of her panic attacks over the phone for two hours in 1999 and another one she had in 2001, I am convinced that about an hour or so before she died, she had a panic attack during which she could not think or figure any way out after sleeping through the work day. [By the way, an instructor Patty had at CSM, Irene, told me Patty had more than one call-in chance for sick days]. Yes, many times I wish God had given me the opportunity to be there to help Patty out of the panic as in 1999 and 2001, but how could I interfere when she was done with her work in life?

We are not in control. We are dependent on God as this event reminds us. It humbles us. That is the irony of death. Man's pride is crumbled and in that death new life blossoms or blooms. Watch life. Be aware of all the places where death gives way to life: seeds, butterflies, spiders, some bees, and Jesus' death revealing to us resurrection of human life.

When we die to ourselves in little things (being unselfish), we contribute to life in the universe. This dying to ourselves should help us see our connectedness to other human beings. Because of our connectedness we should act "in love" for each other. Thus, we should give our love without bias or prejudice.

Patty's life not only showed me "love" for what it is, but my fondest memory of her is that she accepted people as they were. In spite of her own self-doubt, she did not have a need to "look down" on other people who were different.

Patty's greatest tribute was at the funeral when a fellow nurse said no patient was "too little or too least for Patty" - grumpy old men or a dementia patient. Patty treated them all compassionately. This tribute echoes Mt. 25:34 - 40 when Jesus said, "Whatever you did for one of the least of these brothers of mine, you did for me."

My last opportunity to talk to Patty was Tuesday, June 21st, during her lunch break. I told her about dad's emergency knee surgery on Monday evening (MRSA infection) and that he'd be at Elmbrook Hospital until sometime on Wednesday, June 22nd. I gave her the room number and phone number at Elmbrook so she could call dad's room and speak with him. The whole time I spoke with her about what happened to dad's infected knee, she reacted with compassionate moans and groans (as she always did with her bunnies and Cream Puff).

She called dad at the hospital that Tuesday evening from a pay phone as her new cell phone was charging up - his last conversation with Patty.

I thought I had "let go" of Patty in 1997 when she left home for Marquette. I was actually happy she wanted to be independent because as a small child, she would often ask us if she could live with us forever. Now in 2005 I really have to "let go." And I really struggle with this. I keep kicking and screaming inside that I don't want to "let go." But how can I question a God who gave me Patty as "pure gift?" How can I not give back what He gave to me? Somehow I must salvage memories of her that will change how I live my life in a new, improved way. Somehow I must put into action all the platitudes I've believed in for so many years.

Yes, Patty was selfless and yet had self-doubt. In our humanness, we can sometimes doubt, but let's strengthen ourselves by remembering God is always with us.

If the human parents can greatly love their children through "thick and thin," through the good times and the bad times, so much more does God always love His children through the happy times and sad times. And as parents forgive, so does God forgive.

Our life is not over because Patty seems to be gone; but our life should be better because we experienced her.

I feel Patty by my side and still tell her I love her. I now refer to her as my "Patty Power:" my intimate connection with God.

Patty told me on April 20, 2005 that she did not have the faith I had in order to overcome her anxiety about work. But she did have faith. Hers was a faith in God inside people.

Remember, I ask Patty every day to find you a wonderful marriage partner to love and marry.

Death does not sever the bond of love. And it is important to let Patty know we do forgive her. This is important for her to grow on her side and for us to heal on this side.

Love,
Mom

My second letter to Jeanne:

October 14, 2005

Dear Jeanne,

This is a summary of some important intuitive experiences I have had with Patty. I know I expressed these stories many times but am not sure if you were present each time to hear them. They are precious to me in my memories. I hope you will take some time to meditate on each section.

On June 22, 2005 when dad and I were waiting for the police to come to our house, I knew Patty was dead or the police would have sent us to a hospital. I stood in front of Patty's high school graduation picture and said to her in my mind: *I know you are here in your Spirit, right by me. You have got to let me know every day of my life that you are okay and happy.* I do think she started to do this right away as we made decisions in regard to her death. She helped me think clearly so I could ask the right questions of the right people that evening and the next day.

My really dramatic experience of being touched by Patty happened the day of the wake and funeral. On Sunday, June 26, 2005 as dad drove the van to the funeral home, I sat in the back holding down items for the display so they would not fly around and get wrecked. I really got sick to my stomach back there. When I got to the funeral home, the funeral director was very nervous talking to me before we viewed Patty the first time. When I entered the room where Patty was, she looked like she was sleeping on the couch or her old maple twin bed as I walked up to the coffin. Then I looked over her body close-up and started to feel so bad about the large wide bruise on the middle of her forehead, the black freckles on her nose, her swollen neck, swollen arms, and dark finger nails. In my mind I started to question whether it had been a good decision to show Patty. But in an instant, I got an answer which was: *it will be good for her young friends to stare death in the face. Death is a reality that we cannot wish away. This funeral of Patty must testify to that truth.*

Then I wanted to touch Patty but I did not want to kiss her face because I wanted forever to remember what Patty felt like whenever I hugged and kissed her very soft, warm body with vibrant life in it. So instead I grasped both her arms and tried to cradle them in my embrace. When I did that, a very strong sense of peace and calm came over me as though I turned into a completely different person. There were no more stomach-butterflies or sickness - instead immense happiness for Patty. I know it was Patty letting me know she was all right and that I need not worry about her anymore.

Then during the first few days of July I had felt a strong awareness of Patty's presence with me. When I got out of bed around seven-twenty in the morning on July 6, 2005, my mind got a very strong message of: *I'm okay, mom. I have no pain.* In August I again had several weeks of feeling a strong presence of Patty. It almost started to sadden me because I wondered if what I felt was normal. It was then that I struggled with my inside feeling of not really wanting Patty's death to be a reality.

Then I finally thought through the idea that it would be so wrong to even wish Patty back here in this awful life compared to the hereafter. How could I morally even consider asking her to re-enter the mind torture she endured here? Here is when I tried harder to have compassion for what Patty was living with in her mind. I began to understand better the way Patty perceived her life, very different from the way we perceived her life. She did not experience the same confidence in her life that we thought she should have because of how capable she was. I believe she suffered much more than we will ever know in this life. I also believe that now she sees things as they really are and realizes that things could have been worked out and problems could have been solved with communication and support from us and professionals. But she is already happier and in a new form of life. So it is simply up to us to handle our grief and pain and live life *meaningfully*. I do believe Patty can help us do that by helping us understand that she is okay where she is now. In the reading I have done of other suicide victims, half of the survivors' grief seemed to exist around not knowing why their loved one was a victim of suicide. We were so fortunate to have Patty's note. Even though the reading of her note still gravely effects me, I am so grateful that Patty wrote it to all of us.

It was after this kind of thinking developed in me, that I could finally get back to a more personal relationship with God. I never felt angry with God over the situation and don't know if I ever will. I do know I felt a bit numb, but always knew God was there for me, though I could not understand what was happening. But that's life - always a bit of mystery to it. The author of *A Grief Unveiled* says: "Suffering is the heat that softens our hearts." He also maintains that in grief there is a mathematical equation that pain/grief/suffering equals intensity of love.

Another story I love to remember was an example Jacquelyn Oliveira gave in one of her talks. She spoke of a man who found a cocoon in his garden. It was just starting to open. So he helped and finished opening it and then placed the caterpillar-butterfly in a protective container. About three days later it died. The scientific knowledge than given this gardener was that he should have let nature run its course. The strength it would have taken the caterpillar to very gradually open his cocoon himself was the very development he needed in his body later to survive. She then compared this to humans working through the painful process of grief. Once we have a significant loss, the grief work develops strengths in us that we need to survive or we will always be in a cocoon that imprisons us.

In my wonderful little *Emerald Book of Faith* there are two quotes that I think apply to our family after Patty's death. 1. "Faith does not fear change, but knows that all change is simply the spirit's way of moving our life in the direction of our destiny. 2. Faith empowers me to leap across the chasms in my life and to have the confidence that I'll make it to the other side - and to believe that the other side exists."

I wish and pray for your happiness and wellness.

In the Love of God,
Your Mom

On December 16, 2005, I wrote *Open Hearts* at five-thirty in the morning in Puerto Vallarta, MX.

Open Hearts
Hearts are places for permanent memories.
Patty, we stay united in our hearts and our love.

Hearts are places for intangibles.
Patty, we stay united by the drawings you *artistically* created,
the words you *eloquently* wrote,
and the ceramics you *beautifully* molded.

Hearts are places of the Spirit.
Patty, we can communicate in our thoughts,

in our minds, and in the Spirit of God.

Hearts are places of genuine solid convictions.
Patty, we are connected by our belief in God,
in eternal life, and in the everlastingness of our faith.

Hearts are burial grounds of joy and sorrow.
Patty, help us bury the pain of no longer hearing your laughter,
and replace it with the joy you are experiencing now.

Hearts are places for compassion.
Patty, give us some of your sensitiveness
to perceive how others feel and think
to understand their needs.

Hearts are places of good and bad decisions.
Patty, steer us in the direction of good decisions
that reach out to other people.

Hearts are places of listening.
Patty, help us hear each other.

Hearts are places to guide our awareness of the meaning of life.
Patty, help us act on that awareness.

Hearts are places to explore feelings.
Patty, we feel your presence and your love.

Hearts are places to encounter God's creations.
Patty, we recognize you as one of God's created gifts
and continue to see you in the beauty of His
other gifts that we still enjoy.

By Lois Severson

Perhaps the order of these writings appears to be scattered or out of sync. But they are an example of how the grief process progresses and then regresses in a continuous cycle. The following entries come from my reality journal. The hard stuff of grief is not a joy ride of fiction. Grief does not take you on a thrill ride of make-believe.

My advice to grievers: write. Writing can be a great release of pent up feelings and grief. It enables me to let go instead of cling, to forgive instead of harbor a grudge, to have an outlet instead of withdrawal. It frees me.

Some Journal Entries

February 16, 2006
Dear Patty,

This morning I had a wave of grief and crying when I got up. I do feel guilty about April 20th, 2005 (even though last June when you died, I didn't think I was guilty). In our conversation that day I had said, "Your career comes first over volleyball and friends." I was inferring you should slow down to get control of your life schedule, not do so much, so you could get some decent sleep. But I was not perceiving the real source of your anxiety. I am so sorry I could not see the real cause. Instead I thought you were anxious because you were over-tired and in a strange house to sleep and would have to go to work in a couple hours after not sleeping. I do regret not delving into some elaboration of your comment about work "that there was never any down time." Everything was always intense and needed focus.

I really feel bad about this and of course, I can't change it. Just as I many times told you to trust God to allay fears and anxieties, I must turn to God for that now.

As I cried and told Patty I really wanted to be there with her on June 22, 2005, she put in my mind, *"It would have been too much for you."*

Patty, I'm grateful you did not endanger anyone else when you jumped. You were an unselfish person.

April 20, 2006

The day I've been dreading: the one year anniversary of my conversation with Patty about her anxiety at work. She also was confused about how CSM counted sick days and worried about her own record of days. I encouraged her to talk it over with CSM and get it straight.

I got myself to a decent point today to realize I can't take responsibility for not questioning Patty more. If I had dug further I might have gotten into control issues and part of her life she didn't want to share. I wanted to let her have her own life, not me running it.

One good thing I said to Patty was: "You know you are loved, don't you?"

Patty answered: "Yes." Then we gave each other a hug.

The day was long as I remembered all we did a year ago, when she came from work (because they were doing work in her apartment in Cudahy), how she couldn't sleep, her crying, our talk, her calling CSM to come in at eleven instead of seven, her finally falling asleep, her shower here, and then leaving in her cute hat, dressed for work.

The Scripture for today helped me so much, Luke 24:45, "Then he opened their minds to understand...." Lord, open my confused mind. Help me understand. Why couldn't I have thought to suggest to Patty to see a psychiatrist during her time of changing positions at the hospital?

April 21 - 23, 2006

I planted six evergreens on the border of our lot in memory of Patty: for her twenty-seventh birthday on April 29th.

September 24, 2006

Dear Patty,

After doing my 1 Corinthians Bible study out on the patio and admiring God's beautiful creation, I missed you a great deal, cried heavily, and had to read some of the wonderful messages from your great friends. I know what a wonderful person you are. We all should have let you know that more often when you were still with us physically.

Don't forget to stay by our sides, helping us be unselfish, people of integrity, and cheer us up to be people of joy.

Thank you for the neat reminders you sent our way, like today when I looked at the receipt from the store when I bought some cards, the lady who served us at the cash register was Patty S.

I love you! Help me do worthwhile, meaningful things of value. Give me energy. Help me see God.

Love,
Mom

P.S. As I think about some things I've read about suicide, I can't buy everything about what some say about suicide victim's regretting the suicide. I would guess the only regret is that you now know people would have helped you work out the "missed work day" and issues could have been clarified and communication made clearer. Since we can't change the circumstances now, I hope and pray and send my love and energy to you to grow into God, to have happiness, and to keep on being "our Patty Power," helping us whenever and wherever you can in our lives.

Help me be efficient at using your money for needy people and not for ourselves. Help our investments do well so we can give more money to the needy. Take special care of all the little children in the homes we delivered to in 2005 and 2006.

April 18 – 19, 2007 Midnight

Patty, I thought so much about the night at the morgue, June 22, 2005. I listened to the medical examiner and did not go in the smelly examining room and actually see and touch you. I now wish I had gone to your earthly body and kissed your beautiful face one more time. But I suppose I was not strong enough at that time to do it, with the unbelievable shock of your death. I sure wish I could hug you now. Hug my heart with your Spirit.

Grief is like an infection. It can be fatal if ignored.

I believe the following piece flowed from Patty because the urge to write was a driving force. I had to get out of bed at two-thirty in the morning on February 12, 2008. Because we were in the Dominican Republic, I only had some scrap paper on which to write. The words flowed. My physical writing could hardly keep up. The words were pouring out naturally without pre-meditated thought.

I Grieve

I grieve: sometimes it tries to overwhelm me.

I love: without question.

I hurt: it's worth it (no pain - no gain).

I relish: every thought, dream, and reminder of Patty.

I remember: the blessing of giving birth to her.

I marvel: at her compassion, meekness, kindness, and unselfishness.

I see (sense): her in daily events.

I wonder: could it have been different?

I accept: her decision.

I wonder: was it her decision?

I feel: her Spirit - her presence.

I hunger and thirst: for answers.

I drink: the cup of suffering.

I eat: morsels of wisdom in Scripture.

I understand: death is a mystery.

I believe: Patty is happy.

I know: resurrection is hers.

I abhor: the superficial lip-service of some people regarding suicide.

I value: people, life, and living.

I survive: on family, friends, meditation, a personable God, and Scripture.

I imagine: Patty's free Spirit ministering to Bob, Jeanne, and me.

I touch: her Spirit daily.

I play: in and with nature.

I soak: in the beauty of the sea and sky.

I savor: sunsets.

I garden: hoping to learn of growth and transformation.

I glimpse: cycles of life.

I perceive: we are powerless.

I surrender: control and credit to God and others.

I give: up my way.

I pour: out self.

I lift: up my thoughts and mind to God's providence.

I raise: my consciousness to dwell on God's design for the whole universe.

I sleep: with God and Patty in my heart.

I gain: learning and love from this loss of Patty.

I search: for meaning in every event.

I yearn: for peace (within and without).

I discover: new meaning in the most ordinary.

I study: to gain knowledge about suicide.

I meditate: on death, dying, and our next stage of life.

I ache: for the end of tedious time (relativity).

I suffer: with all humans.

I think: suicide may be a natural culmination of illness for some people.

I forgive: all.

I expose: my past for healing.

I restore: positive attitudes/outlooks.

I resolve: to help others.

I vacation: to gain a new perspective.

I write: to express truth.

I find: most things put in perspective need not be stressful.

I satisfy: myself on the spiritual aspects of life.

I pray: lifting my thoughts to an energy level within and above, hoping to find God.

I comfort: the bereaved.

I live: in God.

I trust: nothing can hurt us if we are in God.

I ground: myself in the presence of God; his universal well-being comforts me.

I dwell: in another universe/dimension.

By Lois Severson (Patty)

March 2, 2008
Today's Gospel was John chapter nine about Jesus healing the man born blind. Patty, I think of you being blind to your own goodness, abilities, and wonderful life. I thought of my blindness not seeing how serious your panic-condition, anxiety, and possible depression were. I should have been more assertive and recommended you get professional help back in April, 2005 as you were going through the transition of moving apartments and changing from nights to days into a new surgery position. I

should have recognized this as an anxiety producer (like exams in college). I should have given more credence to the celexa you took in 2001. The oversight on my part makes me readily encourage others to get professional help, but to be sure to give that professional feedback, especially if the medication makes things worse or has major side effects so it should be changed.

March 9, 2008

Raising Lazarus from the dead was today's Gospel reading. This meant Lazarus would have to die a second time: quite a challenge. "Come out," in the Scripture story is telling me to "come out" of my tomb of grief. That tomb is becoming very comfortable. I actually find a security in Patty's Spirit. I can still find comfort in that dimension during meditation and periods of solitude, but I need to break out of that tomb during interactive living and focus on acts of charity. Listening to Jesus' command, "Unbind him," I must also allow myself to be unbound and set free. "God, unbind me from my grief. Help me live free of it by being happy for Patty."

March 22, 2008: Holy Saturday

Two years ago on Good Friday I saw the strong connection between Jesus' suffering and Patty's suffering. In both I could see pain, abandonment, despair, submission, surrender, and death. Two years ago on Holy Saturday I interviewed the married couple who found Patty dying in Cudahy on June 22, 2005. Their witness to me helped me control my imagination when I showered and would envision the re-enactment of Patty jumping, falling, and dying in my mind.

March 23, 2008: Easter Sunday

As I compared the nightmare of Good Friday becoming the joy of Easter Sunday to the nightmare of Patty's suicide, I began to see my pain and grief turning into joy over her resurrection as I become more aware of her presence in my life.

Just as Jesus destroyed the "fear" of death by showing us in his resurrection that death is really a birth, so Patty's death and her revealing resurrection to me has taken away my "fear" of death. My fear is overcome by a yearning for this new kind of birth to a new life.

April 9, 2008

Much grief going to bed tonight: usually I'm quite serene at bed time touching Patty's Spirit. But tonight was different as I relived Patty's anxiety and how I felt I let her down in the discussion on April 20, 2005. I asked her to forgive me as I forgive her. It was a guilt trip down memory lane.

April 20, 2008

Three years ago I had my last talk with Patty about her anxiety. At church today when we prayed the "Lord, have mercy," internally I could throw myself into this vulnerable pit asking for mercy on my inadequacy in not helping Patty more three years ago. Why didn't I say: *Go for help. Are you sure nursing is the right career for you? Are you satisfied with your decision to move to days?* At the time I thought I needed to hang loose and not try to control her life so I only made suggestions, which did not seem very effective.

June 21, 2010

Thanks, Patty, for teaching me about death, dying, and resurrection.

Today's Gospel: "Do not judge." We have all judged incorrectly victims of suicide, but not anymore.

June 22, 2010
Dear Patty,

So hard to believe that today is the fifth anniversary of your resurrection.

Father's Day was so close to this day that it always triggers connections to you as dad and I look at old cards from you and Jeanne. As I went through the box of memorable cards, I found your Mother's Day greeting from May 14, 1989 (fourth grade). On the back of a pink piece of scrap paper, you wrote: "I love you mother. You're the sweetheart of my life. Will you help me with everything that happens to me?"

Yes, I sure wanted to do that, but I was a bit handicapped on April 20th, 2005 when we talked together at home. I wish I would have been more aggressive, but I thought you should be the one in control, not me.

Your question at the end of the above note brought a tear again today. You always had a very touching way of saying things on paper. I so much wish you would have let us help you on June 22, 2005 by calling us when you panicked upon missing the day at work by sleeping. We would have helped you through it.

Reading your question now made me wonder if I'm supposed to help you now with something. What is happening to you now? Can my energy of thought reach you? I hope so. We love you, dear, and miss you so much. Tears flow too readily now. But we did make it to Cudahy today, your physical location of transformation. Then we joined the rest of the family at St. Joseph Convent Chapel for your memorial mass at four o'clock. Aunt Anne played the organ. Then we all went to Omega for dinner and a toast to you. It was good to end with family. I know you are happy and at peace now. Help dad and me and Jeanne be at peace. Help us gain some joy over the fact that you are happy. We need your help to stay focused on Grandpa's house.

Help us get it fixed up. Please send a qualified buyer who can pay for it.

August 13, 2010

God's grace and Patty's Spirit brought a single mom and her three children back into our lives. Her panic attacks and prescription for celexa makes me think Patty sent her into my life to give me the opportunity to nurture someone similar to Patty. I got a very strong sense of this when I pushed hard to get this lady out of the rent debt she had. It became a direct connection to Patty. I was able to be decisive, get her help, and feel confident that I did the right plan of action for the lady and her family. *Thanks, Patty, for helping me see the light. I am resolved to add this family to the list of people I ask you to help daily.*

After all my entries above addressing "guilt," I finally was able to analyze that the person who feels guilt after a family suicide must in some way imagine that he/she has the power to control the victim. Once I related guilt to control, I could surrender my guilt honestly without feeling I was in denial.

I'm okay admitting my daughter was a victim of suicide.

I'm okay being the mother of a suicide victim.

Patty let me know she is okay on her side of life.

All of this is okay because we cannot control each other nor control events. We can only control our response to events. So without guilt we can accept people as they are and events as they occur. This is surrender to the reality of life.

Tracing my grief, I can observe that at the start (June 22, 2005) shock was protecting me. As it unraveled, the pain became worse and worse. Eventually my mind was so preoccupied with the tragic event of Patty's suicide that it seemed it was my daily fare to eat, drink, think, and sleep. Nothing else was important or of interest.

Part of me was analyzing her manner of death. Another part of me wanted to touch Patty's new life and discover what it was like. A sign of my healing after the seventh anniversary is that this need to know and uncover is less burdensome. I am more at rest and content. I can actually laugh out-loud now. I have discovered a richness of life that makes every moment significant and meaningful. Wellness is on the horizon. May this be an example of hope to all who grieve.

CHAPTER 4

Our Gift: Patty

It's a fine line between remembering the
past and dwelling in the past.

P atty was afraid of life sometimes but not afraid of death. So many
other people are *not* afraid of life, but they are afraid of death. At
great financial expense, they cling to life on machines. Was Patty's life
and death teaching me to be willing to embrace death when it comes
for me? Patty is our family's John the Baptist. She is *preparing the way*
for our passage across death to life.

In Luke 1:41 it says: "When Elizabeth heard Mary's greeting, the child
leaped in her womb." I treasure this verse because I felt the conception
of Patty physically in my womb on July 15, *1978*. Furthermore, my labor
pains to deliver Patty began during a Scripture homily on April 29, 1979
in church. She was born four hours later. The priest who had given the
homily teased that Patty was responsive to the Word of God. Indeed
she was a very sensitive person who wore her heart on her sleeve.

As I reflect on her birth, childhood, and years at home, I think of those
years as "heaven on earth" with the love of my husband, Bob, and our
two girls: Jeanne and Patty. Both girls loved sports and excelled in
their schoolwork scholastically. Both decided to go into medical fields

because of the need there and because of not wanting to be teachers since they saw me working at home on schoolwork all the time.

Natural childbirth was an ecstatic experience for me. The thrill of participating in bearing life and watching a miracle happen made childbirth exhilarating. Patty was a very cuddly kind of baby, loved hugs, and got the name Lover-Dover from her baby sitter. Jeanne was delighted to have a baby sister. She wanted us to have a bunch more. We told her she would have to have her own babies some day.

When Patty was eighteen months old, she had a convulsive fever. Her temperature went up so rapidly, it created rigidity in the base of her brain. She had a seizure in her sleep and she stopped breathing. In our bedroom I could hear her body tapping the baby mattress. It woke me up about five in the morning. I was frantic, but Bob kept his cool and gave her mouth- to-mouth while I called emergency. Two police cars came immediately and took Patty and me to the emergency room where our pediatrician gave her a spinal tap to eliminate spinal meningitis. She was hospitalized. It turned out she had a certain type of staff infection. She had to take a liquid barbiturate, phenobarbital, for a two week period. I always worried about what effect such a drug (a depressant) would have on such a small baby. She had another episode a year later and had to repeat the barbiturate for two weeks. These incidents always spoke to Bob and me that we were not the ones in control. We were vulnerable. God was the Power of Life and we were dependent on Him.

When Patty was five, she was afraid to start kindergarten. She cried and said: "I don't know how to read." We told her the other kids didn't either. That's why you go to school: to learn reading and math. That's why we all go to school. After she got to school, she loved it and reading became a passion of hers. She could not put down the books. By fifth and sixth grade she entered the Battle of the Books contest. The first year she came in second and the second year, she and her team won the top trophy.

Just before entering second grade Patty was playing trapeze in the basement on a metal bar from a jungle gym. She slipped and flew way out beyond the carpeting and landed on her face on the cement floor. Two of her teeth went right through her skin below her lip. She was in shock when she came up stairs to tell us. Once she was in the kitchen it started to bleed like a gusher. That scared everyone. So we made a trip to the emergency room for stitches.

During these school years, one very fond memory I have of Patty in first and second grade is how she'd come home on the bus in winter time and forget to come in the house. I'd worry where she might be. When I'd go look for her, she was either lying in the snow making snow angels or walking on the crusty snow that mounded over the top of our three-foot garden fence, prancing all over the snow that was drifted above the garden. One could see how she was enjoying the winter wonderland, our country yard, garden, evergreens, orchard, and field. We had a large forty-acre mini-farm so the yard was spacious.

It was wonderful that the girls could grow up in the country as I did. With very unusual circumstances God had provided our little farm. I say this because we had been on a two-month deal on a four bedroom home in a subdivision while I was selling our eight-family apartment building. When our rental building sold and closed, we took that money to buy our home. However, the home seller recanted on our deal. He was in financial trouble. We only had ten days to vacate our apartment building and find another place to move into. We found this forty-acre mini-farm that had just come on the market and moved within ten days. We thought we would only live there two years, then sell the house on four acres, and keep the extra land for an investment for our children's college educations. God knew what was better for us. We loved the place so much that we stayed thirty years and raised our two children there. We always said to each other that God knew better than we did what was good for us. We are waiting some years yet to be able to say that in regard to Patty's transition from this life. We are sure there are lessons to be learned in this regard.

Patty was an animal lover. She was very compassionate and kind to animals as well as responsible in caring for them. When she took horseback riding lessons, the owner of the ranch said she was a very relaxed and natural rider and did not have a fear of the horse. She wanted to have her own horse, which we considered. We had the space to keep it on our land. However, when Jeanne got thrown by a horse, we thought it would be too dangerous for a hobby. So we got a cat, joined 4-H, and started rabbit breeding.

Oh, did Patty love the rabbits! She not only cared for them with great love and compassion, she would sit out on the silo platform and hold a rabbit and our cat while reading a book to them. Bob loved watching this scenario as he cut the grass every summer. Sometimes she would hold an adult rabbit and our fifteen-pound cat on her lap on the patio to pet them. I thought that was remarkable as our cat in earlier years used to kill wild bunnies and bring them to me like a trophy. Patty would make and design her own birthday cards for the cat and the rabbits. She wrote stories about them endlessly, like a diary on each one. This writing and time spent with the animals turned out to be a refuge for Patty when life was not treating her well. She could always find solace with them. In the summers of her elementary-school years she would set up a wire corral in the back yard, bring out the bunny cages in a circle, and take one bunny out at a time to exercise. Many summers were spent at the county fair, winning ribbons and trophies for her bunnies. One year she received first in rabbit showmanship. Several times her bunnies received first in show.

Other 4-H ribbons she won were for her ceramic pieces of art and charcoal drawings. Her art work is a reminder of the hard work and the one hundred percent effort Patty put into everything she did. Patty's drawing of a horse and colt won a blue ribbon at fair. Her drawing of a dog and cat sleeping together won a red ribbon. The bunnies were expressed in art by making wood cut-outs of each bunny and painting them with the bunnies' names. These wooden bunnies were hung on the cages at the county fair to identify our bunnies. The girls also painted each bunny on the ceramic block wall of our milk house where the bunnies lived with the cat.

Patty was a great collector of toys in her early years: stuffed bears, care bears, pound puppies, pound purries, Sylvanians, little ponies, and ceramic dolls.

Another neat memory I have is how Patty loved Dairy Queen's hot fudge brownie sundae. Whenever we would take her sister, Jeanne, to the orthodontist, Patty would get this sundae at the Dairy Queen next door. It was one of Milwaukee's original ones. It only had a window from which to place an order. So you either took it to go or sat on a picnic table in summer or in your car in fall.

An early sign of Patty's anxiety happened in seventh grade. In one class they were evaluating student writing in groups of four. Patty did not have to share her paper that day but a friend of hers had to submit hers to the group. However, her friend had not completed the writing assignment. Patty felt sorry for her friend so she gave her finished assignment to the friend to read out loud to the group. That evening about ten o'clock, Patty came downstairs from bed crying and unable to sleep. She was worried about the next day when she would have to read her own paper out loud. People would surely recognize it as the paper her friend had read out loud the day before. It would then look as if Patty was the one who had not done the assignment. Even though I said I could help her explain this to the teacher the next day, she was not satisfied. Before Patty would go to sleep, I had to call the teacher at home and explain the situation.

When she was little, sometimes we called her "Grandma Zander," after my mother, because she would sometimes say these wise little things that you would think my mom would say. Actually, on May 15th, just a month before she died, she was home and was giving us some well phrased wisdom on relationships. Bob and I both thought she was going to be okay. But she had not yet started her new position at the hospital.

In fourth grade for Mother's Day, Patty wrote this note to me: "I love you mother. You're the sweetheart of my life. Will you help me with everything that happens to me?" In 2010 during the week approaching the fifth anniversary of Patty's resurrection, I found this original note she had printed. That last question really burned in my mind as I thought of the day she died and how I would have loved to have helped her that day.

I can still hear her "Hi, Mom," greeting whenever she came home and entered the kitchen, whether in grade school or later years when she came home from sports or waitressing.

Volleyball and basketball were Patty's favorite sports. Patty loved to play volleyball. She was on school teams for the sport from seventh grade through high school. In seventh, eighth, ninth and tenth grade she was a setter and sometimes one of the captains of the team. Every summer Patty went to volleyball camp at a different university. In her junior and senior year of high school, a totally new male coach apparently did not like her because he gave so many inferior players more opportunities to play than Patty. Naturally the more those players got to play, the better they became. So in her junior and senior years she hardly got to play at regular games. I finally told her as a senior that it would be okay if she quit. She would have more time to study and work as a waitress. She said she would stick it out as she still got to play volleyball at all the practices every night after school and she liked all the girls on the team for socializing.

At the end of her senior year, the athletic director of the high school told Patty that she would receive the award for the highest grade point average on the volleyball team. He said she could expect the award to be a wooden plaque or a medal. Instead at the awards dinner, Patty received a heavy piece of paper acknowledging the highest grade point average. The coach's favorite player on the team got three huge eight-by-ten wooden plaque awards. However, Patty never complained about this and always loved to play volleyball whenever she had the opportunity. At Marquette University, Patty always played intramural volleyball at the rec-plex building and also played in adult volleyball leagues all over Milwaukee. When she died, she had about a dozen championship shirts from adult volleyball tournaments played in class A.

Another humiliation Patty had in high school was National Honor

Society. Her grade point average was 3.933. Patty was invited as a junior to join, which she did. Then half way through the year she was suspended from the group because of not attending enough of their meetings. But get this: the meetings were during the school day. Because Patty had volleyball after school, a great deal of studying to do, and a waitress job, she would forget to attend the meetings. I thought this was a very strange reason for her to be eliminated, but we all lived with it. But then I noticed there were students in the group who were pregnant and students who drank alcohol and smoked. So when Patty was a senior I suggested to her that she write a letter explaining her objections to being eliminated from NHS in light of other students' infractions that were over looked. She was then reinstated into the National Honor Society as a senior at the next induction ceremony. This is a typical example of how so many groups and honors are really hypocritical.

In addition to the earlier mentioned similarities to John the Baptist, Patty lived a certain austerity in her college life. We had the arrangement with our children that they would pay half of their college and we would pay the other half. Grants and scholarships would go toward their half. Patty came out of four years at Marquette University with no college debt in May, 2001 due to grants, scholarships she worked for, and part time jobs. When I would make food trips for her during her junior and senior years to save on money at Marquette, I always marveled at how hard she studied. She would leave the dorm room or apartment to study in the library or a quiet corner in the union. During her college course work, Patty never touched her savings invested in mutual funds. These funds were started when she was a baby, using gift money from her baptism, birthdays, first communion, confirmation, graduation, etc. When she died, this fund was still intact, growing daily.

She finished a bachelor's degree at Marquette with some grad school work in four years and finished a registered nurse degree in an accelerated program at the University of Wisconsin, Milwaukee in two years. In 2001 she switched from physical therapy at Marquette to nursing at UW. At Marquette she had a 3.785 grade point average and graduated Magna Cum Laude as a member of Alpha Sigma Nu: the honor society of Jesuit Institutions of Higher Education. At UW, Milwaukee in accelerated nursing, Patty had a 3.834 GPA and was always in the Honor Program. She said Marquette courses were always more difficult.

While at Marquette, Patty continued the outdoor activities of camping and downhill skiing our family had done over the years. She joined Avalanche Outdoors Club to go on camping trips and three Western ski trips between semesters. She became the best skier of our family.

When Patty was a junior at Marquette taking her first semester exams, I witnessed a panic attack Patty had about eleven in the evening. She called and said: "I'm so glad you're home." She then proceeded to hysterically talk and cry at the same time about a philosophy exam she was to take the next day. It would be her last exam for which she needed to write an essay on her philosophy of life. She said she was prepared for the two hundred multiple choice questions, but she did not know where to begin with the essay. I was confounded as Patty was a much better writer than I was and in college I would always wing the essay and just write it off the cuff.

I asked Patty questions hoping to stimulate some thought, but she could only react hysterically and could not answer simple questions of mine. She was totally irrational. I certainly did not think I was talking to Patty. So I asked her to get the syllabus of the class from the beginning of the semester and read the course requirements to me including the essay criteria for the exam. When she came back to the phone and read the syllabus to me, she calmed down. I could then ask her questions, get her answers, and develop an outline with her for the essay. We had a good discussion for two hours. When we were finished, she said she would write the essay from the outline before going to bed. I requested that she call me when she finished the exam the next afternoon. When she called the next day, she said that she not only wrote out the whole essay, but memorized it before she went to bed. Then the next afternoon when she went to the exam, she sat down and wrote out the whole essay first, then answered the two hundred multiple choice items, and left the exam in an hour. She told me later she received an A on the exam and an A in the whole course.

To help Patty with this anxiety, we purchased a package called: *"Attacking Anxiety Program"* from the Midwest Center for Stress and Anxiety. It consisted of tapes, videos, a manual of study sheets, and summary flash cards to use as reminders. At first it really seemed to help, but I think eventually when she was very busy, she would forget to use it and practice the program.

The next panic-depression type situation I experienced with Patty was after her Marquette graduation when she was doing graduate work in physical therapy. She was living in her own efficiency apartment on 15th street about a block away from her boy friend. On Friday, September 14, her sister, Jeanne, brought Patty out to talk to us. Patty felt physical therapy was the wrong choice since they now required you to do the diagnosis and an assistant did the therapy. This was not the scenario she thought she was signing up for when she entered the program. She was upset and thought we would also be upset because of Marquette's high tuition. We assured her we were okay with this. She could quit and figure out some other career. She already had a degree if she wanted to get a job or study something else. Bob and I each gave examples of how we had changed our way of life when we were younger. I explained how I had tried real estate part time while teaching. I had also changed from formation in a religious order to lay life and from teaching in private schools to public schools. Bob gave his example of changing from being an electrician to elevator mechanic. Bob also shared how in his last two years before retirement he had experienced panic attacks. We had no problem with her situation and told her to take time to figure out what she wanted to do. We told her the decision to discontinue physical therapy was a lot better than continuing at a very expensive tuition in something she did not want to do.

Because it got late, both Jeanne and Patty slept at home overnight instead of going back to their apartments. Patty's bedroom was right above ours and I could hear her restlessness all night as her bed would creak as she rolled around. Finally I decided to go upstairs and console her. As I got to the top of the staircase, Patty was at the top coming down to the bathroom. We hugged each other and while we were holding each other, Patty said, "I thought when I would tell this to you and dad that I would feel okay and not stressed. But I don't feel any different. I have no will to live."

That last statement really scared me and I had to release my hug and look at her because I was afraid I might tremble and maybe she would feel that in my arms. When she came back from the bathroom, I tried using the Bible, just opening it and reading a passage, as sometimes that worked for me in such situations. We tried it several times but nothing seemed to work for either of us. We talked a while. I can't believe I did not think of praying an "Our Father" together. I usually did this in dangerous situations over the years with the kids. That would have been a good reminder to Patty to resort to prayer during periods of anxiety.

These were the only signs of mental illness I ever saw in her. One of Patty's print-outs said that very emotionally average people have *panic attacks*. It also said only ten percent of these people are victims of suicide. More recently I read an article that said it this way: "A recent study suggests that, tragically, one out of five sufferers attempts to end his or her life, never realizing that there was hope and treatment available." Notice the statement says "attempts."

This same article that Patty found on the internet September 20, 2001 said: "Now we regard panic disorder as more of a physical problem with a metabolic core. It is not an emotional problem, although after suffering from it, emotionally healthy persons may develop depression or other problems. There are different theories about where in the nervous system the problem exists.

"There is considerable evidence pointing toward abnormality in the function of the locus ceruleus and its associated nerve pathways. The locus ceruleus is a tiny nerve center in the brainstem (the part of the brain that controls heartbeat, breathing, and other functions).

"A few experts still cling to the notion that this is not a physical disorder. The overwhelming opinion by the experts is that scientific evidence clearly favors there being a physical cause of this disorder. It is regarded as a physical disorder much like diabetes or pneumonia." Patty had also told me she had learned that over-production by the adrenaline glands was involved.

After the September 14th night discussion, I helped Patty exit Marquette studies and discontinue tuition. Patty then spent the remainder of the semester taking career counseling and used various testing instruments and interpretations to figure out what she should go into for a career. She also saw a psychologist and received two prescriptions, one of which was celexa.

In our Christmas card that year, Patty wrote this note:

> Dear Mom and Dad,
>
> Thank you so much for all the support and help you've given me since I left PT. It was the hardest decision I've ever made thus far, and it could have been a lot worse if you were upset with my decision. I couldn't have done this without you. And though I haven't found a job, I think it was probably for the best because I've been pushing myself so hard for the last four years, with work and school, so this is a nice break for me. I really feel I've grown and learned so much about myself because of this experience. Thank you for sticking by me in my search and selflessly helping me.
>
> Love,
> Patty

During this half semester off school, Patty chose nursing to study. She found out UW-Milwaukee was the best rated nursing school in the state, checked out which of her courses at Marquette would transfer for a registered nurse degree, took fourteen credits of additional requirements during second semester, and then registered for the accelerated nursing program at UW-Milwaukee. She completed this program in one and a half years with honors.

Upon graduation in nursing, she received a bonus to work nights on the ortho-med floor at Columbia St. Mary's. She thought the night schedule would work for her because as a student she was used to being up all hours of the night, studying or going out. But something none of us knew (learned it later from a friend who works nights), this kind of night work leads to great anxiety. Our friend said this anxiety stayed with him for two years. A regular sleep pattern did not happen for him until two years into that schedule. Patty worked this schedule for a year and a half. I did not like how the pattern of nights worked. She would often have three nights in succession of seven in the evening until seven in the morning. Then they would consult with the next shift of nurses coming on and write up note reports for an hour and a half. So it was usually eight-thirty in the morning before she left work and could then do errands on the way home, get sleep, and be back to work by seven in the evening. She frequently had trouble sleeping because of anxiety. She said it was a job where there was never any "down" time. One always had to be alert and focused. Because she was usually tired she would drink lots of caffeine drinks to stay awake and focused. As a result, too much of this caffeine was still in her body when she would try to go to sleep at home. So she'd lay awake and be worn out when it was time to go back to work. Sometimes the time she would fall asleep was close to the time she was supposed to go back to work. So then she'd call the hospital to see if someone could take the first four hours of her shift. At other times she, too, would take an additional four hours of work for someone else after her twelve hour shift, which turned it into a sixteen hour shift. I not only saw the toll this schedule took on Patty, but I do not see the logic of why we are doing this in our medical system where it is very important for people to be alert in order to make good quick decisions. Some doctors, (I discovered from a friend) take thirty-six hour shifts during internships. How absurd! (Don't give me one of those doctors).

On April 20, 2005 I was able to see first-hand the toll this routine was having on Patty. After she had moved into her new apartment in Cudahy, April 17, 2005, the management needed to do some work in her apartment. Patty was still working nights and assumed she would not be able to sleep while they hammered in her living room. She drove to our house, arrived after nine in the morning, and tried to sleep. By two-thirty in the afternoon, she had not slept yet and was supposed to be at work again by seven. She came out of the bedroom and was crying, anxious about not getting any rest. Not being in her-own bed did not help the situation. She must have also found out that day before leaving work that there was something she did not understand about the way the hospital counted sick days used. I told her to talk to someone and ask all her questions to see that she understood things properly. I did not think I should get involved except to give her advice. She also talked about never having down time at work; things always had to be focused. I tried to tell her some mind games I used to work on myself when I was teaching, hoping to take some emotion out of the situation. Regretfully, I mentioned that she might have to give up some time with her friends in order to get enough sleep because her career came first. At this time I did not sense a need to ask if nursing was the right career for her. At the end of our talk, I hugged Patty and said, "You know you are loved, don't you?" She answered, "Yes."

My thought was that nursing was the correct profession for Patty because she was unselfish and compassionate. During her first month at work at the hospital, she had a dementia woman recovering from surgery. The woman had trouble speaking. Usually she could barely get one word out. So when she needed something, she could only scream in her pain from surgery. Patty said that sometimes other nurses would just walk by that lady's room ignoring the screaming. Patty would go in to her bedside and try to move her pillow around or put the bed up or down, trying different things that might give the lady some comfort. Patty said this would sometimes help the lady get a word out to communicate what she really needed. One time Patty said the lady got a whole sentence out by using this method.

After one and a half years of this night schedule, Patty thought working the day shift might be better so her life with her boy friend from Chicago would work out better, hoping she would quit falling asleep on their dates during the day. The only position open on the day shift at her hospital was a position in surgery, which would take nine months of strenuous training. As we found out later, this was too soon in her nursing career to progress to this position. Change was always difficult for Patty, but once she got practiced in something she'd love it. Unfortunately, during this change in work position (which involved a change in sleeping hours), she also moved her apartment a further distance from work (from one mile to fourteen miles). So there were really three changes going on here in her life: apartment change, nights to days, and ortho-med floor to surgery. None of us thought to tell her to see a doctor about anxiety. But she was (at the time of her death) trying to make an appointment with a psychologist. By the list of doctors on her computer table, I could see she had already called some of them. She had also asked her surgery instructor at work how a nurse on days made doctor's appointments, since doctors only worked during the day. Her instructor was going to get back to her the day she died.

After leaving for college, Patty developed many friendships at school, volleyball, and work. When she died, she had three hundred names, addresses, and phone numbers in her palm pilot of people with whom she kept in touch. Needless to say she had a large funeral, but those from out of state could only send e-mails or cards. At age twenty-six she had affected the lives of many people in a good way.

As a result of these friendships, there were always too many social events to attend. When her boy friend, Steve, would come up from Chicago, he wanted to just spend time with Patty. But she would have four to six places and events lined up so he would have to wait for the end of the evening to be alone with her. It reminded me of a song by Kenny Chesney about living life "fast-forward, need to rewind real slow."

On May 15th, 2005 we had lunch with Steve and Patty. They were cute together. After lunch they were going to pick up Patty's new round dinette table and four stools for her new apartment. They seemed so natural and in love. I felt she was secure. I knew she loved Steve. But I forgot she had not yet started her new position at the hospital.

Patty lived life to the fullest, giving her whole heart and soul. She was not pretentious. She was an unselfish person and in that way she had fulfilled her purpose in life. As Iain Provan put it in his book on Ecclesiastes (I studied this book four years after Patty's death): "Our human vocation is to love God, to love our neighbor, and to look after the earth, not to take advantage of the order of the universe to engage in self-centered and manipulative living....Cause and effect only get us so far, e.g. if we pursue good things such as health and education as an ultimate value, they will only disappoint us in the end. For beyond cause and effect, there is God, who will not allow the idolatry of the self ultimately to exist."

Patty was unselfish when she was misunderstood. She would just plain "take it." Often she would not defend herself or make excuses. A typical example was when a fellow waitress told her one could order anything from the cooks and get the food free. She explained how she did it so Patty followed her example as this person had worked at the restaurant longer than Patty. When Patty ordered an omelet from the cooks and ate it during her break, she was reprimanded by the manager, told she would have to pay for the omelet, and if she ever tried that again, she would be fired.

Even as a youngster (after third grade) in the summer of 1988 at a family reunion, she was a visual example of unselfishness to me as I recently watched the video tape of that reunion. All the cousins were taking turns riding a quarter-horse around the farm. Patty absolutely loved horses. She was not first. She did not get a turn in the middle. Near the end, she was getting on the horse, had one foot in the left stirrup, had her hand on the saddle and was about to swing her right foot over the horse. Just then someone yelled out, Patty got down from the horse, and another cousin got on the horse. Then Patty became the absolute last cousin to ride the horse. As I watched that tape a second time, I thought: *how typical that incident was of Patty's life.*

In Patty's last Christmas card to us, she wrote: "Thanks for always being there for me!" I save this card.

When Patty died, she had my last birthday card to her on her computer table. I had chosen the card because part of the verse had said:

On this birthday,
May you feel proud of your life

And excited about your future
As the world celebrates
The wonderful person you are.

I then wrote to her in the same card:

In meditation ask Jesus to show you *your great personal worth and value.* That is why Jesus came to earth. We were not understanding God's creation, especially ourselves in relationship to Him. But if we study the human and divine Jesus, we have his example to learn from. Ask Him to teach you faith, give you faith, especially faith in yourself. You are a great person! He loves you and we love you! God (Jesus) is the greatest psychiatrist. He has given us His Spirit to dwell in our hearts. Touch Him in your own heart. Discover Him there. "We are restless, until we rest in God."

Another card from Patty that I saved was the last Mother's Day card she gave me six weeks before she died. In the card, she put an arrow bracket by these words:

For as long as I can remember,
the first person I turned to in joy or trouble was you
you always seemed to know exactly what to do or say,
no matter what the situation,
and I'd feel reassured by your confidence.

Next to her bracket, Patty wrote me this note:

This is so true. Thanks for always listening to me and talking me through things when I was in despair or anxious. You've always been there for me and I just want you to know how much I appreciate it. I know I don't thank you enough but I want you to know I couldn't imagine having a better Mother than you!

Thanks with love,
Patty

After I read this, I wanted to ask Patty how things were going after our talk of April 20th and ask if she had communicated with work about her sick days. But we were not alone so while others occupied the conversation for a minute, I told her how I liked the note and that I wished I had been more aware of her anxiety when she was living at home. She replied that she had been okay then. The anxiety problems had come later at college. I never had another opportunity to talk alone with her confidentially.

In her death I remembered Patty had the heart of a great adventurer. In one of her high school English papers called *Taking a Year*, Patty wrote:

> With all of the pressures of the present day, many people try to get away from it all. If I could take a year off and do with it what I pleased, I would travel. I would sail to Australia. This trip would get me away from all of the pressures of today as well as the people who cause them. I would try things that I have never done before.

As a matter of fact, I would do things that I have never thought of doing before. I would learn to scuba dive, to see all of the tropical, aquatic life that is part of a world that is totally foreign to me.

Another foreign world would have to be the sky. I would have to learn how to fly or free fall. Maybe I could sky dive or bungee jump. The only problem is that I would probably have to be physically pushed to do these things. So maybe I'll have to settle for a hot air balloon ride.

Obviously, these are all things that the average person would not attempt to do. And one thing is for sure, I am one of those people. These stunts would be completed not by me, but the great adventurer inside of me. I would be able to say that I quenched my thirst for adventure by sailing around the world, and spending the better part of a year on the other side of the world doing wild and sometimes crazy things. That would be a year I would never forget, definitely not a waste of a year.

Patty, in her junior year of high school, did spend a month in Australia and New Zealand to fulfill part of that adventure. During her freshman year at Marquette University, she did sky dive one weekend. On a summary at the end of that year she listed as the scariest thing she had ever done in her life: "jumped out of a plane."

Her favorite quote that same year was: "If you love something, set it free; if it comes back to you, it's yours; if it doesn't, it was never meant to be." And Patty was set free.

On her memory card we had one side saying: *Going Home...*(with a graphic of a flying dove). On the reverse side we printed: *I'm Free.*

CHAPTER 5

Confirmation of Life

"I have come that you may have life and have it more abundantly."
John 10:10

A round April 29th, 2008 (Patty's golden birthday), Fr. Brian's wife was packing for their move to Fond du Lac. She came across an old box of Brian's, opened it, found a manila folder on top, opened it, and found a fire orange-red piece of stationary on top that was signed: Love, Patty. She wondered if it was our Patty. Upon checking with Brian, he confirmed that it was Patty's confirmation letter from 1996.

Patty's Confirmation Letter: she was seventeen when she wrote it.

> Dear Jesus,
>
> I would like to be confirmed. I've been in religious education since I was five. My religious education has been a good experience for me. I've learned a lot from my teachers about God and what he wants for me. But I think my best experience has come from my family. My parents instilled good values and a deep knowledge about God in me. I come from a very religious family, as I'm sure you know, so I think I've really become close to God.
>
> I am now sixteen, and am preparing to be confirmed. A part

of the confirmation program is doing service hours. This was a very good experience for me. I've done a bunch of it in the past, but when you're with a group of kids your age, it becomes very special. Serving at St. Gall's was a great experience, because I was aware of how fortunate my family is and how sheltered I am from many of the problems in the world. It also gave me a good feeling to help those people.

We also started our own program at Church, called "Helping Hands," in which people in the community ask for help in some way. We went to homes of the elderly to change storm windows, wash windows, and rake leaves. It was a lot of fun, and I felt good about helping people.

I also was a bell ringer during Christmas time at K-Mart. And it was more fun than I thought. I got to spread some Christmas cheer and meet some really nice people.

My best experience though, was my retreat this year. For once, I could talk about my beliefs and see how God is part of every aspect of my life. I met a lot of great people there that I'll never forget. It was a really great experience that anyone who's gone would understand.

I made a creed I'd like to share with you. *I believe that Jesus loves us completely, and with this love he forgives us, no matter what we have done. I also believe that God has been with me from the beginning and he will always be with me, especially in tough times.*

I like the parable about the house built on rock. If we are really committed to God, we will let nothing destroy that. But if we are not completely committed, things will get in the way, and we will lose God in our hearts. I don't believe I have become fully committed to God yet, but I am working towards it, so my confirmation is a true experience.

I promise though that I will always believe you, and you will be the center of my life. Religion is nothing without you as the basis of it. I realize how hard it must have been for you to die for me and all mankind. This is so impressive and amazing that I believe I will always be committed to you for it.

Love,
Patty

Recently I found the letters my husband and I wrote to Patty to be opened at her confirmation retreat. Then I found her letter she wrote at retreat to us in response. The three letters follow here.

November 9, 1995

Dear Patty,

This is a great opportunity to say some things that are in my mind and heart many times. First of all, I love you very much! Sometime I wonder if I love you too much. By that I mean, sometimes it makes me over zealous for you when I become too concerned about you and your welfare to the point of becoming impatient over a situation because I want something to turn out just the very best for you. The second meaning I had in the above statement of "too much" love is that we probably spoil you a bit. But maybe that's okay as the world does a good job making reality set in when things get hard.

I also want to use this letter to tell you how sorry I am that I am not a perfect parent. I do try to be as good as I can, but I know that I'm human and don't always do things right. For that I apologize. But I want you to know dad and I try very hard for your well-being and welfare. That does make me feel good because even though we haven't always been one hundred percent correct, we have discussed problems and family things together a lot so as to brain storm and come up with ideas that will help our family. That's where I feel dad and I have been good parents because we have a partnership that makes decisions and plans together.

I also want to tell you that you personally have always given me loads of joy and opportunities to be really proud of you. You do not only have academic ability for me to be proud of but also sports ability and a very pleasant personality. Continue these strong traits and you will always be successful and happy in life.

I'm also very proud of you in that you have a strong belief in God and prayer. That will help you very much through "thick and thin" times of life. Always work hard at your faith life. Faith is a gift from God, but it can also be developed by you. I hope this retreat will help you firm up exactly what you believe in so you can mature in the faith and values we've tried to instill in you. By that I mean that you as an adult can say: "I believe in this…..and I value this…."

It's very good, for instance, that you at times take the Gospels or Scriptures and read about them or meditate on them yourself. That is another good quality about you: that you recognize that such a habit is good for you morally and psychologically.

We are praying for you at this retreat that it will be a faith building experience for you and at the same time fun.

I hope someday in life you will have the experience I had today. I was very tired and depressed after this past week and I did not feel good this morning when I got up. I really felt the need to pray, but not just pray at home, a real need to pray in a community. So Mass this morning really helped me have a good day and get things straight again in my mind.

You probably think: will mom ever get done writing? But I have one more thing to tell you. I'm really happy how you are getting more aggressive about your own life. For example, the way you approached Davian's yourself for the raise and the way you talked to your teacher about your chorus grade. That's the same thing you'll have to do in college so it's good you're getting practice now.

Good luck to you in choosing a career, college, and a way of life. Big decisions are coming up (worth praying over), but you are showing that you are capable of making them.

Also, good luck on your Student Ambassador endeavor. We pray for your success in that, too.

We've always been happy with your achievements in 4-H, National Honor Society, and contests, but most of all we hope you will put faith and religion on the same pedestal as something "great" to achieve.

I love you very much!

Mom

November 10, 1995

Dear Patty,

I have loved you all your life through good and bad but with much more of the former.

It is such a great joy to have children that don't have to be pushed to do homework and take pride in themselves to always become the best they can be.

You know right from wrong and we trust you to make the best decision in all cases.

It is great that you have chosen to be confirmed and with God in your life nothing can stop you from becoming the person that you want to be. I will be proud of you no matter what you choose to do with your life as long as it makes you happy. You must remember it is your life and no one elses.

Patty, you must never be afraid to talk to your mom or me. If you make mistakes, we will always be there for you no matter how bad it may seem to you at the time.

I know that I am very rough on you at times, but it is only because I want other people to love you as much as I do.

My love is forever,
Dad

Patty's reply from retreat:

Dear Mom and Dad,

Oh my god! I had no idea you guys were going to do this. When I got to the Church, people were handing Dot their "love letters," but I didn't connect it at first because I thought my envelope was for Dot to help her at some point during the retreat.

But anyway! I loved what you wrote. I almost started crying when I read them. It doesn't seem like we get to talk much because we're all so busy. So it was really great to know all those things and how you feel about me.

I love you all so much. And I know you all know that, but I really don't get to say that too much. And like any parents, you don't always to the right things. But neither do I. I think you're doing a great job. You're always helping me get things done or give me advice when I'm struggling with problems.

I smiled with pride at all the things you said you were proud of me for. It really makes me feel good to know that you feel that way. I don't think I've realized how many accomplishments I've had.

I think the best thing you guys do is never get really upset when I act stupid or do some bad things. You know that I'm going to screw up and you accept that. You don't blame me, but help me to know better next time. I think this shows a parent's love is there through the bad times.

This retreat has been a really good experience for me. I feel closer to God and I want to do more for people who don't have all the things I have. I hope I can live like God wants me to, and have patience with and respect for all people, because everyone has a gift to give. Thanks for all the values you've given me and support.

Love,
Patty

The following is a letter from me that Patty had saved in her scrap book.

Christmas, 2000

Dear Patty,

It not only is a special Christmas, being the year 2000, but the reason I am writing this letter is that I have a Confirmation candidate whose name I have to write faith letters to and am praying for special this year. I figured if I am writing her faith letters, I could write one to you, too.

As you are on your own now, you are affirming your own faith in God and life values as an adult, no longer having dad and me to verify you as a witness to Christ's presence in the world. Yes, our heritage of beliefs we passed on to you was and continues to be important to you. But now you are assuming (taking on) all of that heritage (or inheritance) within yourself and saying: "Yes, I want this; I believe in this; I can be Christ to the world; I can serve the way Christ served by using the power of His Spirit within me."

As you continue to study your faith and grow personally in it,

I think you will find solace, inner happiness, and peace within. It will be a happiness or satisfying completeness that no one on the outside can ever take from you. No matter what happens to you on the outside, no one can take away your relationship with your God.

I hope you are growing in your prayer life, making prayer a very personal talking to God in your own words from the heart. As one grows in prayer over the years, one realizes it is not always getting exactly what we ask of God that is good for us. God has the big picture so sometimes our prayers are answered when we don't get what we want and we can really see that God's way is better than our way. When we tried to sell our apartment building and buy a regular house, real estate deal after deal fell apart until by very short notice (ten days) we were able to buy our forty acre farm that you grew up on. At the time, we only thought we would stay here two years and move on; but in God's big picture, we have been very happy as we complete our twenty-sixth year here. So we pray to Him and are patient in our deal to sell the farm now as He sees better than we do.

Many similar decision making situations come up in your life, too. Pray over them, be still, and meditate over big decisions and God will inspire you even if it is through discussions with other people whom He provides for you.

My greatest hope and wish for you is that you will always grow in your relationship with God, and that this relationship will be more important than any other friends or friendships that you may experience. In fact, I pray that by building a relationship with God, it will impact your other relationships positively.

My last thoughts for 2000: 1) when I die, I plan to be by your side in Spirit with Christ and guide you to do good and make good decisions; 2) always, always remember: no other drugs but alcohol and enjoy alcohol in moderation if you want to have a life free of depression and loss of memory.

To a happy life in 2001,

P.S. Prayer card enclosed. Pray it frequently.

Love,
Mom

Bob and I wrote this letter to Jeanne for New Years, 2009

January 1, 2009

Dear Jeanne,

One of my year end meditations gave me this idea: instead of a bunch of New Year's resolutions, write a letter to a loved one, seek forgiveness and offer your love as a way to clear any roadblocks and heal any wounds.

So when and if anger ever tries to consume you, save this letter to read in order to calm yourself.

Starting with Patty's words of "Please forgive me," Dad and I ask you to "Please forgive us" for any times we unwittingly caused you pain, were too hard on you, or demanded too much of you over the years. Our love for you and Patty is so great that sometimes we went overboard or over the edge in our endeavors. One of the beautiful things about Patty's death is that we learned first-hand that this family bond of love cannot be destroyed by death. That bond of love lasts forever and exists in the present tense "today," right now.

You are the apple of our eye and Patty's. As such, the love from the three of us should lift you up above controversy, conflict, and the trials and struggles of this life. Learn from this love to exist in God Who is love itself. When you love and are loved, you experience God.

My night prayer to Patty has been to ask her to find you a loving partner. My prayer now is that IF _____ is that partner, I ask Patty to help your relationship grow in love, trust, and unselfishness. If these traits of integrity and faithfulness exist in your relationship, you will both be happy.

If one person should break the trust, the other should not retaliate in a spirit of revenge. Revenge only results in poisoning oneself. Reconciliation and forgiveness should take over.

Our youthfulness is gone; old age has set in; but wisdom does prevail.

We love you and treasure you!
Mom and Dad

CHAPTER 6

Blindness

"I lay down my life of my own accord...." John 10:17-18

References in the Bible for this chapter are:
Blind Man John 9: 1 - 41
Bartimaeus Mark 10: 46 - 52

In society we are blind to our bias about suicide. Just as cultures and organizations have to struggle with race, religion, and equal rights for women we still struggle with viewpoints on suicide. We have only scratched the surface of this topic. We treat the topic with avoidance and omission. After all it is a sad topic, not your usual chosen cocktail or dinner topic. It does not engage us unless our work involves it or it touches our lives by happening in our family or among our friends. Once it happens to us, it becomes our *reality show*.

Even in grief circles it is amazing how absent it is. It amazed me how I had to search for sources myself. Almost six years after my daughter's suicide, I finally found and purchased two Care Notes on suicide. My church's bereavement ministry, of which I was a part, had been a source of many different Care Notes, but not one of them was specific to suicide. Needless to say I purchased ten of each suicide Care Note so I could give them to families experiencing suicide.

In reading the two Care Notes, I was surprised that I recognized many things I just naturally did after Patty's suicide. It made me grateful God led me on the right path to deal with this special death. I embrace this path. I cherish this path. My life must be different because I have traveled this path.

So much I've learned and unlearned. One concept I threw out the window and "unlearned" was the past teaching by the church and society's general view of suicide. Reading that helped me do this was every book on suicide I could lay my hands on and Fr. Ronald Rolheiser's annual article on suicide that appears in the Catholic Herald (usually in the month of August). His emphasis is on suicide being an illness, not a sin. Many people see mental illness as a stigma. This leads the people who suffer with it to think less of themselves and others who are afflicted with it.

In my fifth year of grieving I became a bit angry with institutionalized religion and society for imposing on all of us such a moral window regarding suicide. I feel anger over the taboos, shame, and mind set on suicide that they instilled in us. It is comparable to Catholics thinking they are the only ones in heaven. How dare we (church or society) tell God how much mercy and love he is allowed to dispense. Is "Divine Mercy Sunday" only a pretense, hanging out there like an ad but not really lived? "The Lord is gracious and merciful, slow to anger and of great kindness." Psalm 145:8

So many fundamentalists like to quote scripture about Judas' suicide and condemn him. Yes, he was a betrayer, but even scripture has a different scenario in Acts 1: 16 - 19 as well as some early church oral legends. Only God can judge. How do we know whether or not Judas' death was not an act of remorse with corresponding forgiveness? Only God knows. In my own mind I clarify that we do not know what went on between God and Judas in his transition from this life.

Over the centuries, I believe churches and society tried to discourage people from committing suicide by imposing such negative parameters on suicide. Churches thought people would not commit suicide if it was called a sin. When "mental illness" was not even a vocabulary term, Gospel stories would portray people that Jesus healed of mental illness as people who had demons. Furthermore, in American history as shown at Williamsburg, VA, one can see cells where mentally ill patients were imprisoned and chained to their beds. No wonder people wanted to hide mental illness when they were treated in this manner.

But to impose punishment for suicide on the victims or their survivors is not the way to prevent suicide. Someone thought fear would work instead of instruction and education on mental illness. At one time some states even had civil laws against it, maybe some still do. As a result suicide victims through the ages were buried outside cemeteries. Things of course have changed, so to shun such historical practices, I keep Patty's ashes in our home, not allowing anyone to tell me where or how I am supposed to handle this.

As a survivor of my twenty-six year old daughter's suicide, I find these negative parameters abhorrent, ridiculous, and lacking of understanding of mental illness and disease. Churches and society are still very "blind" when it comes to the topic of suicide. This is true because our other daughter, Jeanne, broke down and cried when we were planning Patty's funeral with our priest. She cried because she did not want her sister to be in hell because of a suicide death. She had learned this, unknown to me, in high school religion classes as recently as 1990 - 1994. Father explained God's forgiveness as existing before we do anything wrong and we had a discussion on God's great mercy as a Father.

In addition my "Little Black Book" for Lent of 2006 had a meditation the fifth week of Lent on this Scripture: "Then Jesus said, 'Father, forgive them, they know not what they do,' " Luke 23:34. Luke's writing is saying that Jesus is talking about God forgiving *before* repentance is even expressed. And what better Scripture could I quote to express what goes on when a person succumbs to suicide: "They know not what they do."

I'm sure I still exhibit signs of blindness about suicide due to biases taught to me by religion and society. When my life was touched by the suicides of former students and a teacher friend with three children and a neighbor mother with two children, I had a glimpse of the mystery surrounding such deaths. But I was still blind to signs that could have led to constructive help for my own daughter. However, I will not go so far as to say that I could have prevented Patty's suicide. I make this statement because we cannot control another individual, even God does not do this. God gives us free will. In the volumes of reading I did in libraries and book stores, studies have shown that what saved one individual could not save another. Medications did not always save and in some cases caused the suicide. Hospitalization did not always save an individual. Recently I read the notice of a young man Patty's age who committed suicide while being hospitalized for help. It appears to me that we cannot prevent all suicides. Once I reached that conclusion, I decided to go through my own guilt trip faster. I did not think I could completely overlook my guilt for fear of not facing reality or being honest with myself. But I could plow through it and not let it overcome me. My main way of addressing my own guilt was to journal my feelings about the guilt and by rereading Patty's letters and notes in which she acknowledged my understanding.

My issue with religion and society began to gel when we had the blind man reading the fourth Sunday of Lent. The story reminds us about "humanity" being born blind spiritually, how Jesus heals the man born blind (helping humanity "see"), and how the religious leaders of the time refused "to see," even though they claimed they were not blind and could already "see." So many times society and our churches exhibit blindness, but claim they can "see" when it comes to understanding suicide.

How many times in life as a math and science teacher I thought I did see, only to learn in the death of my daughter, that I was very blind and so were many people around me. Jesus opened my eyes in Patty's death.

When people call suicide a sin, they are just like the Pharisees in the man born blind story. The Pharisees emphasize the point that Jesus is breaking the law of the Sabbath by healing the blind man. Jesus was not breaking a law but was being compassionate. Likewise, I do not believe Patty broke any law when she was a victim of suicide. God is the judge, not humans.

As our family is going through the healing of our blindness now after Patty's transformation to resurrection, I feel very much like the blind man going to the educated leaders of his religion, telling them he "sees" more than they "see." In the church I have found several very understanding, compassionate priests regarding suicide such as our pastor and the priest who had Patty's funeral and certainly Fr. Ron Rolheiser. These people are rare. Too many priests and lay people are still brain washed by the past teachings and practices of religion and society regarding suicide. Yet there are so many others who fear the topic, run away from it and its survivors, and do not like to talk about it, as though hiding in a box surrounded by silence on the topic will magically make it go away. I will not react that way. I will break the silence by acknowledging suicide as a presence in our lives. I will not pretend that it did not happen because it did. I did not want a private funeral for that reason. I wanted to be honest with everyone about how Patty died. The shock *that she died so suddenly and that it was by suicide was a double whammy.* I could not hide something so devastating.

In my reading about other's experiences with suicide, I gained some understanding that suicide is just another way of dying, akin to cancer or kidney disease. A friend of mine who suffers from depression explained to me that mental illness is a brain disorder just as diabetes is a disorder of the pancreas. In our past history we have treated mentally ill people poorly by chaining them to beds in prison cells. In the Gospels, Jesus healed many who had demons. Some of these demons were due to mental illness. Jesus had great compassion for these marginal people of society.

This kind of information is important to discuss. But because church and society want us to "hush, hush" regarding suicide, it is sometimes hard to talk to others about it. It hurt me to see others repulsed by the topic of suicide or death. Some people cannot talk about death, much less suicide.

The situation made me think of a Taoist story John Shea tells in one of his books. It tells of a man in a small boat in foggy conditions. He sees another boat coming at him so he yells to make the other boat aware of his presence. The boat keeps on coming. By now the man is so frustrated, he is swearing at the other boater. As the boat gets close enough in the fog, he sees that the other boat is empty and steers around it. This story made me think of how I sometimes felt like the empty boat, meandering along. I saw people trying to avoid me shortly after the funeral. Sometimes I reacted by not staying empty and I steered around them, too. I also find myself steering around people with very set controlling religious ideas, ones who live by mandate rather than the Spirit. I need to adjust my rowing to find a course/direction for my life that will heal and still be purposeful. The empty boat should remind me that an emptied ego is a prerequisite for me to be filled with love. To stay empty my writing must be motivated by an attempt to build understanding about suicide and to help others endure it when it happens.

"Patty seemed so normal," many would say. My own brain toyed with that thought so much of the first couple years. But have we figured out yet that there is no such thing as "normal?" All of us have some imperfections and a certain degree of mental illness. Our brains are not perfect and do not function perfectly. Even the crazy comedians who use suicide in their jokes exhibit their mental illness to the public. I cannot imagine what is comedic about suicide. I believe it is a topic about which we should speak, but not laugh at it. We should discuss it seriously but not dismiss it with a superior "better-than-thou" type of attitude.

Comedians who jab at victims of suicide lack an understanding of human helplessness, feel superiority by cutting others down, and totally don't "get it" that in their audiences are families and friends of *real people* who were victims of suicide. Believe me it is not humorous when someone you love deeply is consumed by suicide. Comedians create a world of shame around the suicide arena, lacking any kind of wisdom on the subject. This lack of sensitivity is very thoughtless and embitters people over the fact that someone makes money being so insensitive. Comedians: consider the topic of suicide off limits.

Side bar: this reminds me of Mark 10: 46 - 52 about the blind man

Bartimaeus. Bartimaeus means "Son of fear." After suicide in our family, I could react by being a daughter of fear. But like Bartimaeus I will not hide in darkness and remain silent. Instead I want to seek light and speak out like Bartimaeus did. Mark 10:48 says: "Many rebuked him, telling him to be silent. But he kept calling out all the more...." Bartimaeus does not hide his darkness, his lack of vision. I will not hide in darkness. I will speak out "all the more" about Patty and how she died. As I speak, I will respond to Jesus' question of Bartimaeus: "What do you want me to do for you?" MK 10:51. I answer: "Jesus Christ, give me sight (vision) on this dark subject, give me courage to look at all angles, and heal me in a way that uses my brokenness for others."

In God's providence, I wonder sometimes, if that is how God is gracing Patty's transformation as a teachable moment for her many, many friends and relatives. It stopped all of us in our tracks, made us look at what is *really important* in life, and made us stand in awe at Patty's kindness and compassion, a reflection of God himself. We had been gifted by her life.

This "blindness about suicide" causes feelings of shame in survivors, making them ashamed about suicide in their family. Here I find great comfort in Jesus' death (almost a suicide since he knew he would be killed in going to Jerusalem). Consider John 10: 17 - 18. "For this reason the Father loves me, because I lay down my life in order to take it up again. No one takes it from me, but I lay it down of my own accord. I have the power to lay it down, and I have the power to take it up again."

I put myself in Mary's shoes and imagine her grief was greater than mine because her son was treated as a criminal when he was innocent. Only slaves and abhorrent criminals were put to death by crucifixion. But even though Jesus endured a death of shame by society's standards, he was not ashamed. In second Isaiah 50:7 in one of the servant songs, it says: "The Holy One helps me; therefore, I am not disgraced; I have set my face like flint, knowing that I shall not be put to shame." These are my words today. I am not ashamed of Patty, nor the manner in which she died. In giving up her life, Patty did not hurt or kill anyone else. Good Friday has taken on a whole new meaning for me. Could the church ever "see" Jesus' death of shame and suicides in a "like" dimension? To me Patty's death at age twenty-six was a crucifixion experience. Patty and I can identify with Jesus and Mary on Good Friday. Jesus and Patty were innocent; Mary and I are the grieving mothers.

On the first Holy Week after Patty's transformation, my husband and I visited the Holy Land in Orlando, Florida. We witnessed a very touching Way of the Cross, crucifixion, and resurrection. On Holy Saturday of that week I spoke with the young married couple who found Patty on the ground as she was dying. I interviewed them, asking as many questions as I could and wrote down their responses. I needed their witness since I was not present for her transformation. For ten months I had imagined her jumping, her grounding, and Jesus raising her up by the hand saying, "Get up," to resurrected life. Those words have become my slogan to "Get up," get going, live life, and take others by the hand to raise them up.

As Patty's transformation taught me more and more about resurrection and assured me of its reality, the passage in the blind man's story that said "He was born blind so that God's works might be revealed in him," makes much more sense. God's work is indeed revealed in Patty's life and her transformation to the next stage of life. As God's Spirit and Patty's Spirit operate in our daily lives, God once again is glorified. There no longer seems to be such a gulf or separation between our worlds. I witness to this truth as I accept and bear what I cannot change. "Not as I will; but as you will," Mt.26: 39. This means I accept the cauterizing numbness, the surrender of well-laid plans, and the necessity to die daily in order to live.

As Gunilla Norris phrases it in *A Mystic Garden*:

> *Continuing to ask questions*
> *is a way for the mind to make itself important,*
> *to pretend it has control.*
> *Let go.*
> *You are dying daily.*

CHAPTER 7

Contributing Factors

"God takes you to the depths of your being – until you are at rock bottom – and then, if you turn to him with utter and blind faith, and resolve in your heart and mind to walk only with Him and toward Him, picks you up by the bootstraps and leads you home."

NBC reporter David Bloom in his last e-mail to his family. Bloom died April 6, 2003, of a pulmonary embolism while covering the Iraq War.

A major difference between Patty and me would be her sensitivity. By contrast I am this crusty seventy-year-old lady who taught junior high math and science for thirty-five years and had many years of lunchroom supervision - a tough job, psychologically. In teaching junior high, I grew tough skin; Patty could not. Do you think I care about what others think of me? No. Do you think I care about helping others? Yes.

It is in this vein that I list some variables that may have contributed to Patty's suicide. But I do not want anyone interpreting this list as a definitive answer for "why?" The list is conjecture as I feel a bit handicapped in dealing with this issue. Why make the list then? Hopefully it will help a reader in a similar situation reach out to others for support and help. Or perhaps it will make a parent aware of signals or signs of trouble.

1. As a baby Patty had to take a barbiturate for two weeks two different times when she had a seizure. I believe this depressant affected her brain.

2. Patty participated in binge drinking on some weekends in college. Alcohol is a depressant. A college classmate's husband was a binge drinker, suffered from depression, and was a victim of suicide.

3. Patty had finished an oxycontin prescription for back pain.

4. Patty had a diazepam prescription as a muscle relaxer after a back injury at work.

5. Too much caffeine versus sleeping pills syndrome affecting sleeping cycle

6. Sleep deprivation

7. General anxiety - panic attacks

8. Depression

9. Cigarette smoking at Marquette while dating a heavy smoker for four years

10. Marijuana use sophomore year of college

11. Changes were difficult for her. Patty had just moved to a different apartment fourteen miles from the hospital instead of one mile. She had changed working nights to working days. This caused a new sleep routine with which she was having trouble. She started keeping a chart on her sleep patterns. She changed from working on the ortho-med floor

to working in surgery. She had just begun nine months of strenuous study for this new position.

12. Patty always approached something new thinking that she was supposed to already know how to do everything, even when nine months of training was involved.

13. Patty was a perfectionist in her seven years of college studies getting two degrees, suffering anxiety at exam time.

14. Involved in too many activities – often scheduled more than time would allow

15. In college Patty told me once: "You always look at things in a positive way; I always look at things in a negative way."

16. After Patty concluded physical therapy was not her career choice any longer in 2001, she told me: "I don't have the will to live." She then took off a half semester of school, saw a psychiatrist for therapy and took two prescriptions: celexa and clonazepam. She went for therapy about one year. She took career tests and began an accelerated nursing program.

17. Nursing as a career: I read that this is an at-risk career regarding depression and suicide.

18. Working the night shift one and a half years was a cause of anxiety. A friend told me that it took him two years to shed the anxiety when working nights and sleeping days.

19. On her computer table Patty had a list of psychiatrists from the internet with names circled of doctors covered by her insurance plan. It looked as if she had already called some of them about hours and had asked her supervisor at work how to make doctor's appointments when one is on first shift.

20. In an old journal I found after her death, Patty wrote of

suicide in eighth grade. At the end of the writing, she said she was okay and got over the idea.

21. Sometimes Patty misunderstood what authority figures said. I think this is true about the sick day discussion she had with those who interviewed her for the new surgery position.

22. Low opinion of herself

23. On her kitchen countertop Patty had a weight loss supplement bottle that she had ordered from a mail order catalog. Dr. Siegel on a Sunday TV segment said these types of supplements can mess with hormones and contribute to anxiety.

24. The weekend before Patty died, she and Steve and a group of friends went river rafting and camping up north. Patty got very tired and no doubt there was lots of drinking. This over tiring weekend and alcohol depressing her further set up the over-anxious Monday and Tuesday working all day and not sleeping at night. Those were her last days at work before she died on Wednesday.

One time when Patty's dad and I were discussing a problem with Patty in high school, she explained that even though she knew what was right and logical, it seemed she had to experience something first and then learn from her mistakes. St. Paul expressed the same thing in Romans 7:15 when he said: "What I do, I do not understand. For I do not do what I want, but I do what I hate."

In her book, *Suicide*, Laura Dolce quotes a study by Jacobson (p.38), who suggested that the administration of barbiturates to mothers during labor might lead to drug addiction later in the child's life. This scared me. If a barbiturate could have such an effect on a baby after going through the mother's body, I assumed it would have even a greater effect going directly into the baby as it was given to Patty for two weeks when she had seizures at only eighteen months of age. When she was three years old she had another seizure followed by another two weeks on the barbiturate.

Before I could put depression on the list above, I had to do lots of reading and consider that statistics say that sixty percent of suicides are caused by depression. And suicides of depressed people, especially depressed males, tend to be more violent. This gave me pause to re-evaluate what I thought was a panic attack during Patty's last minutes because I consider jumping from the sixth floor a violent death; the neighbor across the hall saw her two hours before her death and said Patty looked very sad; Patty had written as a freshman in college that the scariest thing she had done was to free fall from an airplane; and in her last Mother's Day card to me she spoke of her "despair." I was blind, always hoping her love of Steve and working days instead of nights would really help her.

As you can see by the following hand-written letter Patty left for us, she felt helpless.

> *I'm so sorry to everyone. I couldn't handle going on anymore. The anxiety I felt about my career, not feeling like I knew what I was doing was torture. I couldn't think straight, I couldn't function any longer. The littlest things were too difficult for me to do. Pressures welled up inside me; I felt there was no escape. I didn't know how to make things better. Please forgive me. I love my family and friends and apologize sincerely for the pain I am going to cause them.*
>
> *Patty*

Not one word was misspelled. Not one word or letter was crossed out. All was legible. For Patty, living had become a deeper pain than dying.

"Come to me all you who labor and are
burdened and I will give you rest."
Matthew 11:28

As the Portuguese proverb says, "God writes straight with crooked lines." We cannot discern God's mind. So instead of pretending we know "why" this event happened, we have to surrender to the mystery of this act. John Shea phrases it: "We are mystery because we are related to Ultimate Mystery." In spite of the list I made above, Patty had very much positive going on in her life. She just could not see it at the time. In Job 32:8 it says: "But it is the Spirit in a mortal, the breath of the Almighty, that gives him *understanding*." I pray for that inspired understanding daily.

A college classmate of mine who suffers from clinical depression and does not know why wrote this quote to me: "If I insist and obsess about answering the question of why I will come to have not just one life lost, but a second one as well, mine." This was a solid thought that consoled me as I read stories of suicides during or right after hospitalization. There were stories of suicides caused by medication, which really disturbed me. Indeed this is a complicated scenario.

Worldwide for females, ages fifteen to forty-four, suicide is the second leading cause of death, says the World Health Organization. This stat came from J. Raymond DePaulo, M.D. in his book: *Understanding Depression*, p. 133.

Suicide is the eleventh leading cause of death in the U.S. It is the third leading cause of death for those ten to twenty-four years of age. More than ninety percent of those who die by suicide have a diagnosable mental disorder, (NAMI Fact Sheet).

Again Laura Dolce in her book, *Suicide*, p. 49, says: "Many people believe that only mentally ill people kill themselves. While this is true in some cases, it is not the rule. Many (suicide victims are) people who are otherwise viewed as normal but cannot seem to find a way out of their current difficulties."

In the same book, p.32, Dolce says, "People in certain high-stress jobs, such as policemen, lawyers, and health care professionals (including doctors, nurses, psychiatrists, counselors, and dentists), are also at a higher risk of suicide."

At the same time we must remember that just as some cancers end in premature death, some brain illnesses end in premature death. Just as some body systems become ill biologically so can one's brain biologically malfunction due to a chemical imbalance.

Is any one of these worse than the other? Should we exhibit understanding of both and understanding of the people who have the illness? Paul says in 1 Corinthians 1:27, "But God chose what is foolish in the world to shame the wise; God chose what is weak in the world to shame the strong."

I beg the question: are deaths by suicide any worse than people slowly dying from the side effects of their prescribed pharmaceutical drugs? There are many prescribed drugs causing great harm to people who take them with great faith. Many people view their medicine cabinet of twenty to thirty drugs as normal to prolong a life that might be very painful. I have no answer. I only pose the question for thought.

In addition, everyone who listens to the news realizes we have drug addictions from both illegal and legal drugs in our society. To this end I challenge some Hollywood movie stars and society in general: why do you campaign for the environment and at the same time pollute your own bodies with drugs that ruin the environment of your body and soul? This is typical bi-polar behavior. I promote non-pollution of body, soul, and environment.

Perhaps the only way to accomplish a serene acceptance of what we cannot change is to admit: all will die sometime some day. It is a reality of life.

The following paragraph of information came from a pamphlet published by NAMI in Waukesha County (National Alliance on Mental Illness).

Great people who have experienced one of the major mental illnesses of schizophrenia, bi-polar disorder, major depression or anxiety disorder include: Winston Churchill, Abraham Lincoln, Vincent Van Gogh, Mozart, Beethoven, Tennessee Williams, Charles Dickens, Ernest

Hemingway, Michelangelo, Sir Isaac Newton, Patty Duke, Bette Midler, John Keats, Lionel Aldridge, Mike Wallace, Sting, and many others. To state the obvious: "People with mental illness have enriched our lives."

The mentally ill suffer greatly. We make their suffering worse when we fail to understand them. The following poem by Rumi from "The Guest House" in *The Illuminated Rumi* poses with great thought the purpose of sorrow and suffering in life.

This being human is a guest house,
Every morning a new arrival.
A joy, a depression, a meanness,
Some momentary awareness comes
As an unexpected visitor.
Welcome and entertain them all!
Even if they're a crowd of sorrows,
Who violently sweep your house
Empty of its furniture,
Still, treat each guest honorably,
He may be clearing you out
For some new delight.
This dark thought, the shame, the malice,
Meet them at the door laughing,
And invite them in.
Be grateful for whoever comes,
Because each has been sent
As a guide from beyond.

CHAPTER 8

Meditation Pieces

Grain of Wheat
A grain of wheat has to "*fall* to the ground and die"
If it is going to produce "much fruit."
Without dying, there is no *new* life. John 12: 24 – 26

Patty fell to the ground, died, and now experiences new life. As we went to her apartment to remove her possessions and clothing, I grew from abhorrence for the place to a loving affection for the location Patty last touched on this earth. I went from feeling sick to my stomach to a lingering affectionate gaze on her dwelling as I closed the door to her apartment for the last time on July 25, 2005.

After the funeral, our first time back to the apartment was a Wednesday. Bob and I had resolved to look over everything to try to decide where and how to dispose of Patty's things. While Bob was doing this in the living room, I went to her office and started going through bills and business mail to see if anything needed immediate attention. After a short time, I started to feel sick. I looked at my watch. It was five o'clock. This was the exact time one week ago when Patty panicked and jumped. Why couldn't we have been here last week at this time? This week we were here at the exact same hour with no planning. The irony of the thought made me more sick. Just then Bob came into the office and said: "Let's go!" I agreed quickly and we took off and exchanged identical thoughts in the car driving home. We agreed that we would have to make a plan each day on exactly what we could haul and get it out of the apartment quickly to cut down on our time there until we could get used to it.

On the lawn where Patty died, someone had placed a single purple rose with a hand written note: "Beautiful Girl, may you rest in peace."

During our month of having to go to her apartment, I went from staring on this spot with disbelief to gazing with appreciation at the physical location where God said to Patty: "Get up," and raised her into full resurrected life. This place was "the end of the world" for Patty but a new beginning of a very real new life. Even God's natural creation exemplified this new beginning by growing a patch of beautiful green grass where her torso was practically outlined. Her blood on this ground washed deeper by water used for clean-up grew something on this side of life, too. It made me reflect on the blood and water that came from Jesus' side on the cross. His blood and water was also a sign fulfilling all the water and river images in the Old Testament (Jeremiah, Isaiah, and Ezekiel), ultimately teaching us that God dwells with us and is our "living water" sustaining us with His life.

I feel like I fell to the ground with Patty, died to self, and was awakened by a force I could not change. I cannot go back in time. I cannot rewind. I cannot hit the replay button. I do not get a "do over." An inner poverty helps me search for meaning in this event. A very significant message I have realized is that "the sufferings of this present time are not worth comparing with the glory about to be revealed in us." (Rom 8:18)

God and Patty daily reveal a bit at a time to me during meditation and quiet times. But the instant in which I glimpse a small piece of the puzzle is only temporary and beyond my imagination. I thank God for these wondrous glimpses. His big picture escapes us humans because if we were able to grasp it, it would overwhelm us.

John Shea in year B of his series for Christian preachers and teachers on p. 206 says "Jesus' death is conceived as a movement from 'a grain of wheat' into 'much fruit' (John 12:24). It is not a loss, but a transformative process through which He will be more. Part of that more is His increased accessibility. He will be available to more people as the risen Lord than He is as Jesus, the historical individual."

So Patty in risen form is more accessible to all of us than her physical presence ever was. Her spiritual presence makes this possible. Though her spiritual presence is more difficult for us to sense, it is a more powerful presence, capable of so much more than her earthly physical presence was. This teaches all of us to believe in physical death as a transformation to the next stage of life. We need not fear it, but hope for it. We are to remember what Paul said in 1st Corinthians 15:36: "You fool! What you sow is not brought to life unless it dies."

Resurrection Thoughts

"I am the Resurrection and the life: whoever believes in me, even though they should die, will come to life; and whoever is alive and believes in me will never die."
John 11: 25 - 26

This chapter eleven from the Gospel of John used on the 5th Sunday of Lent allows us time to meditate on resurrection, a favorite topic now that Patty lives life in that form. Some of my bereaved friends react to this story with anger, asking why doesn't Jesus bring their loved one back to this life the way he brought Lazarus back? Have they considered that maybe Lazarus did not want to come back to this life? It also meant Lazarus would have to make the transition from this life a second time. Was that fair or delightful? Humanly speaking, I don't think so.

A major point of this Lazarus story is to lead us to believe that Christ is divine and thus has the power to be "the resurrection and the life." In order to reveal His divinity and power, he purposely waited to go to Bethany so no one would doubt Lazarus was really dead physically. As God is glorified in this miracle, we become convinced he also has the power for all of us to experience resurrected life now and more fully when we make our transition from this life. The details of this resurrected life are mystery. Humans cannot fully describe it. Doesn't it stand to reason that resurrection should be beyond our comprehension? After all, we are not gods; it should be beyond our grasp.

Some scripture scholars have thought that the resurrection of Jesus Christ happened instantaneously with his death. Note that the physical body was still there to place in a tomb. So it should not be necessary to claim there was no body in the tomb to preach the Christian concept of resurrection. Even if someday archeologists would find some bones (like in 2007) that hypothetically might be Jesus Christ's bones. Finding his bones does not discount resurrection. Keep in mind those to whom Jesus appeared after resurrection did not recognize Him at first. Mary Magdalene thought He was the gardener at first. The two disciples walking to Emmaus spoke to Him on the journey and did not recognize Him until the breaking of the bread. And notice in the Gospels, they did not see Him all the time. When He wanted to be seen, He either assumed a physical body or made his body visible when He wanted to be seen by them. Those who saw Him were usually terrified. Since Jesus offers us the same gift of resurrection, why couldn't it be possible that our loved ones also experience resurrection upon their transition from this life? Even though their ashes or bones are here deteriorating, they can also have bodies of a new nature in a dimension of life that we cannot imagine or understand. Keep in mind the body we die with is a different set of physical cells than we were born with and grew up with. Our physical cells are changing constantly. We look very different in old age than we did in our young years. Do you think God's resurrection for us is limited to a certain set of atoms? No way! God is so beyond our imagination and design. So in our death which is a transition into a new dimension, why not consider the possibility of change, difference, and newness of a resurrected body?

With God there is no time, so why do we think resurrection can only happen at the end of time? Remember Paul's message to the Thessalonians about the second coming of Christ being very imminent. It turned out not to be imminent in the course of history. So has it occurred to institutionalized religion that we may have misinterpreted the concept of the second coming of Christ? Why would our loved ones have to wait for the end of time to resurrect? God can gift us anyway he wishes. The details of this resurrection are unimportant. We will never know the particulars in this life. We may not be able to understand God's process. But with God, nothing is impossible.

Often Christian teachers use the experience of a baby in the womb not knowing anything of this earthly life until birth as an analogy of how we know nothing about details of life after death. The following was given in a Sunday morning homily to illustrate that analogy.

One day a mother conceived twins. One was a girl, the other, a boy. Weeks passed, and they developed. As they grew, they sang for joy, "Isn't it great to be alive! Isn't it wonderful!" Together they explored their mother's womb. When they found their mother's life cord, they shouted for joy, "How great is our mother's love, that she shares her life with us!"

Well, one day after about eight or nine months, the twins began to feel some drastic changes. "What does this mean?" asked the boy. "It means that our life in our mother's womb is coming to an end," said the girl. "But I don't want to leave here," said the boy. "I want to stay in this place forever." "So do I," said the girl, "but we have no choice. Yet, maybe there is life after birth."

"How can there be?" asked the boy. "We will shed our mother's cord, and how is life possible without it? Besides, there's evidence in the womb that others were here before us, and none of them ever came back to tell us that there is life after birth. No, this is going to be the end."

And so the boy and girl both fell into despair, saying, "If life in the womb ends in death, what's its purpose? What's its meaning? Maybe we don't even have a mother. Maybe we made her up just to feel good." "But we must have a mother," said the girl. "How else did we get here? How else do we stay alive?" And so the last hours in the womb were filled with deep questioning and fear.

Finally, the moment of birth arrived, and the twins thought life was over. But when the twins opened their eyes, they cried for joy. What they saw exceeded their wildest dreams. They saw their mom and dad, and they saw their brothers and sisters who had gone before them. They soon saw aunts and uncles, cousins and many new friends.

And the twins knew at that very moment, that there certainly was life, even more abundant life, after birth.

How similar the foregoing rendition is to a death experience!

In this area of resurrection, I think it might be possible that our loved ones are here among us in resurrected form but we cannot see them. This is Spirit presence. They see all of creation with *new* eyes of understanding and beauty.

The way Patty has touched my life since June 22, 2005 has indeed found reinforcement in the Word of God: Scripture. These references have been of great help for meditation on her resurrection.

Isaiah 26: 19 and 52: 13 - 14

Job 19: 25 - 26

Psalm 16: 10

Daniel 12: 2 - 3

2 Maccabees 7: 9, 14, 23, 29b, 36a

1 Corinthians 15: 42 - 57

Philippians 3: 21

Ephesians 1 : 20

Matthew 22: 23 - 33 and Matthew 28

Mark 12: 18 - 27 and Mark 16

Luke 20: 27 - 40 and Luke 24

John 11: 25 and John 20 and John 21:12 - 13

Acts 10: 41

Revelation 11: 9 - 12

In the Lazarus story we find a present day interpretation when we dwell on the meaning of the words Lazarus and Bethany. Lazarus means:

God helps. Bethany means: the house of the afflicted. In every death scenario that is what God does; He helps the afflicted: the one dying and those who survive the event and feel afflicted.

For me the Lazarus story culminates with Jesus' directive: "Lazarus "(God helps) _____(my name), "come out." This speaks to me inviting me to come out of my tomb of grief. Jesus directs the by-standers to untie him (me) and set him (me) free.

Chapter 9

Scripture Passages Heal Grief

"Then the eyes of the blind shall be opened,
And the ears of the deaf unstopped;
Then the lame shall leap like a deer,
And the tongue of the speechless sing for joy.
For the waters shall break forth in the wilderness,
And the streams in the desert....
Isaiah 35: 5-6 (NRSV)

The Word of God has provided me much comfort, consolation, and insight during my grief process. I ask the Holy Spirit for wisdom and awareness as I pray the Scriptures. It is amazing the insights that come to light when one approaches God's Word unhurried and prayerfully. It is truly "resting" in God. It reminds me of how often Jesus said, "I remain in you" or "I abide in you," in John's Gospel.

There have been countless passages from the Bible that have struck me and caused me to stop in my tracks and say: "Aha!" The passages that I reference in this chapter have all helped me. Either they related to my grief or connected somehow to suicide. In making that personal connection, my pondering then used the passage as solace, comfort, and prayer.

Here are a few examples showing how I did the above. For the passage quoted at the start of this chapter from Isaiah 35, I applied the "blind" to myself. The "see" I applied to the mind's eye and asked to be opened to understand my grief about suicide. "Deaf" I applied to my not listening enough to Patty and other victims of suicide. "Unstopped" I applied to opening my ears to information and tuning in to the speech of others. I asked for the ability to heed my own grief and the grief of others: to listen with full attention. "Lame" I applied to my limping along in sadness after Patty's death. I asked for the ability to walk tall and unashamed: to leap with a joy that Patty would want me to have in life. "Speechless" or "mute" I applied to being silent about the subject of suicide. As I heal, I am resolved to speak out and write on suicide. I ask Patty for her ability to write and ask God to help me use the correct words that will inspire and motivate those who read my writing. The words "wilderness" and "desert" aptly describe the life of exile we live here. "Waters" and "streams" remind me that God provides for us the necessities of mind, body, and soul even when we are unaware of His providence. Our wilderness would be impossible to traverse without His care.

The following references from the Bible helped me in my grief. They communicated to me God's view of my suffering. My favorite translations to use are the NRSV (New Revised Standard Version) and the NIV (New International Version).

1 Corinthians 1: 23-25; 2: 9-10; 7:32; 10:13; 15: 26, 54-55; 13: 8

2 Corinthians 1:3-4; 4: 7-14; 5: 7-8.

1 Thessalonians 4: 13; 5: 8-11.

Galatians 6: 2

2 Thessalonians 3: 16.

Ephesians 1:18; 3: 19; 4:30; 6: 13-16

Romans 8:18, 28, 38-39; 15: 13.

Philippians 1:21; 3:10; 4:6.

Hebrews 2:18; 4: 15-16; 11:1; 12:1-2; 13:5.

1 John 3: 1-3; 4:9.

Revelation 21:4; 7: 14b, 16a, 17.

"I have found in the Bible words for my inner most

thoughts, songs for my joy, utterance for my hidden griefs and pleadings for my shame and feebleness."
Samuel Taylor Coleridge

Mark 4:34-41; 10: 2-16; 14:36

Matthew 5:4; 6:25, 27; 11:28-30; 14:22-36; 16: 25; 17:23; 20: 1-16; 21: 33-46; 24: 42; 26:38; 28: 5-6.

John 6:20, 39-40, 44; 10: 17-18; 11:25,35; 12: 24-26, 32, 46; 13:7; 14:1-3, 6, 27; 16:6-7, 20-22; 19: 25; 20: 13-14, 17.

Luke 1: 46-56; 2: 19, 35, 48-50; 6: 10; 6: 21b; 7: 6-9, 47; NIV 20: 35-36; 22: 42-44; 23: 34.

Acts 24: 15

Lamentations 2: 19, 22b; 3: 22, 23, 25, 26;

Isaiah 25: 6-8; 29: 7b; 30:19; 35: 5-6; 38: 5; 40: 31; 41: 10, 13, 14a; 44: 8; 49: 13b, 15; 50: 7; 54: 4, 10; 58: 8-9; 61: 1-2.

Jeremiah 14: 17, 19; 29: 10-11; 31: 12-13, 15-17.

Wisdom 1: 13-15; 2: 22a, 23-24; chapters 3 & 4; 9: 16; 13: 5; 14: 15-16.

Job 6: 2-3a; 20: 8; 36: 15; 38: 17-21; 42: 3.

Proverbs 10: 7; 23: 18.

Psalms 4: 9; 6: 8-9; 13: 2a, 3a; 18: 2; 22: 1, 11, 14-15, 19; 31: 9; 34: 18-19; 37: 1, 3, 5b, 7, 8b, 11, 23-24, 28; 42: 2-3,5,9,11; 44: 24; 55: 2; 56: 8-9; 69: 1-3, 5, 13-18, 20-21, 29-30, 32-34; 71: 20-21; 73: 21-26a; 81: 8; 88: 5, 15; 116: 3, 4a, 5b, 6-9, 12, 15; 118: 5-6; 120: 1; 121: 1-2; 130: 1-2, 4a-5, 7; 139: 13; 147: 3.

Ecclesiastes 3: 11; 8: 17; 9: 11.

1 Peter 5: 7

Deuteronomy 30:19.   **2 Samuel** 19: 1-4

Sirach 15: 17; 3: 20; 35: 12-13, 18-19.

When reading about an angel or angels in Scripture, remember the Hebrew meaning for angel: "messenger of God." Read the book of Tobit and appreciate the role and example of Raphael accompanying Tobias on his journey and mission. I think of God giving us Patty as

His messenger to our family and her friends. Look for the messengers in your life, recognize them, cooperate with them, and learn from them.

Last, but not least, is the great connection I have found in John Shea's writing about resurrection and spiritual presence in *The Spiritual Wisdom of the Gospels for Christian Preachers and Teachers, Year B, Eating with the Bridegroom*, p. 244. Here is one small sample where John is explaining the Gospel passage in Mark 10:2 – 16 where Jesus is talking about marriage and ends with a passage on little children. John Shea discusses spiritual consciousness: "When we are in our child-of-God consciousness, we have the potential of becoming a giver of our personal spirit into the spiritual identity of one we love. We can also become the receiver of the spirit of another into our spiritual identity. We are not self-enclosed individuals; we are reciprocal love-giving spirits...."

"Childhood and marriage can be understood from social, physical, and mental perspectives. But spiritual wisdom interprets them as symbols of distinctive aspects of spiritual consciousness. We are transcendent beings capable of freely entering into each other's interiority in knowledge and love." These passages explain my spiritual "oneness" with Patty in her Spirit form.

As I am doing my final edit, I had a tremendous insight today when I read John Shea's interpretation of the doubting Thomas Gospel story for the Second Sunday of Easter. John's explanation appears on pages 107-116 of *Year C, The Relentless Widow* in the same book series and title mentioned in the previous paragraphs. I can relate to John's explanation that Thomas will not be able to probe Jesus' wounds because the wounds are not available for physical verification. "These wounds are ones that Jesus shows to people so they may receive God's life and realize His true identity." This is a true mystical experience giving spiritual knowledge of a subtle nature. Jesus' resurrection presence was not that of a resuscitated corpse returning to an earthy existence. The sorrow His followers felt over His physical death is replaced by the *joy* of His spiritual presence. The world cannot give this kind of joy. Everything of the world will eventually end. But this spiritual presence of the risen Jesus and Patty will never end.

How do I relate the above to my grieving wound? In this book I open my wound and my families' wounds for all to see. Our wounds are gifts. They are invisible and unobtrusive, but they are real. Like the wounds of Jesus, we receive God's life through our wounds and realize our identities in His identity. We need to appreciate our wounds and take advantage of all they teach us in the spiritual realm. Patty experiences the same resurrection Jesus does. Thus her spiritual resurrection presence can be just as real, but not touchable. How amazing!

In our home we have a tangible symbol of our families' wounds: an oil painting by Peter Anthony of Jesus showing Thomas His wounds. It is a daily reminder of our on-going healing.

Our wound is healing; each day of acceptance
brings us closer to full restoration.

CHAPTER 10

Good That Evolved

"I believe that nothing that happens to me is meaningless,
and that it is good for us all that it should be so, even if it
runs counter to our own wishes. As I see it, I'm here for some
purpose, and I only hope I may fulfill it. In the light of the great
purpose all our privations and disappointments are trivial."
Dietrich Bonhoeffer

After June 22, 2005, my goal has been to find the meaning for me in Patty's premature transfiguration. It is a daily search for meaning and purpose. I find I must rely on God's providence to live each day. From the start I knew good would flow from this tragedy. Everyone says even though things may look bad, God can bring good from it. It became my job to look for that good. As a result, I have come to believe that we as humans may call or label something "bad." But God knows what is best for us to learn and what we need in order to learn. So when all is said and done, sometimes we may need something rather unpleasant to learn everlasting truth. As humans, we are too cocky and arrogant to "get it" without a good jolt.

One of my first observations was the reconciliation of two of my friends from Metro Bible Study at Patty's wake at the funeral home. I also hoped and prayed that Patty's friends would be influenced to have faith in God because of this death experience or at least be influenced to lead a good life.

In my early reading on death and dying, much was said about people having fulfilled their purpose in life when they die. I began to dwell on this and looked at the reality: Patty had fulfilled her purpose in life. She had been unselfish, compassionate, and had made a difference in her world of influence. In her death, the world now saw her value, her great worth, her true inner and outer beauty, her interest in learning and in others, her talents, her humor, and her ability to reach out.

Patty's death made us stop in our tracks. It makes us examine our awareness of purpose in our lives. It teaches us what is important and what is trivial in life. Hopefully this book will give me purpose and make a difference in society.

Remember: the bad news and pain of Patty's suicide is balanced with the good news of her eternal union with God as she enjoys resurrection. Because we cannot see her in resurrected form, it is harder for us to be joyful about this. However, we should delight in the joy that Patty is now experiencing and be happy for her.

After my three very poignant experiences of Patty's Spirit touching my life, (see Chapter 1), I firmly know resurrection is a reality of our existence. Without Patty confirming resurrection for me, I would not be so certain of it and believe only with faith. Do I know what that life is like? No, but I know it exists. The details are still a mystery.

At first I asked Patty to show me some of this revelation and what she knows of God now. But I have since changed my mind, realizing our human stage of life is too frail, could not understand such mystery, and would simply be overwhelmed with such contemplation. Instead I have decided to study Scripture, hoping to grasp in small steps the revelation God has given us in His inspired Word.

The purpose of our grief I believe is to enable us to grow by reaching out to others. One way we can do this is to comfort and console others who are experiencing grief. In bereavement ministry I help other people cope with the mystery of death. It helps me to have such discussions and I hope it helps others. There is a certain amount of release when one can discuss death and its meaning with someone who shares a similar loss. Too many people are tongue tied on this subject. As a result, early grievers have trouble finding supportive people with whom they can express their feelings and talk about their situation.

In my bereavement ministry I had a special empathy for widows and widowers because their loss created an aloneness never experienced before. A number of them expressed how alone they felt, especially at night. For one widow it helped if I called her in the evening. Through our church I then started a group called: "Companions on the Journey." I would simply put a notice in the bulletin that anyone who lost their spouse was invited for breakfast at a local restaurant. We tried to do this twice a month at first. Often twelve-to-fifteen people attended. After several months I thought I should drop out of the group because sometimes references to my husband came up naturally in the conversations and I thought it might sadden some people. I asked two of the widows to please take over the leadership. They are still meeting once a month at the same restaurant. This has been going on for about seven years.

Spiritual friends came out of the woodwork. I was so fortunate to have many one-on-one lunches at my house with friends who were deeply spiritual. To this day I am able to have such conversations with spiritually based people, friend and stranger. These meaningful conversations really fed me in contrast to hum-drum social settings with lots of prattle. In the first few months after Patty's transition, I only wanted to talk about death, dying, suicide, Patty, and our family. Yet I knew if that was all I talked about, it would depress other people. But that is the world my mind wanted to investigate, hoping to achieve some understanding of this tragedy.

Perhaps the greatest "good" that I experienced was having a husband who would listen to me as I shared thoughts with him from my reading, dreams about Patty, and meditations. Bob was always more quiet in his grief. However, he would discuss things with me if I initiated the conversation. He would also offer his own thoughts on the matter. This helped both of us a great deal. I know for a fact that this is not true for many married couples who have lost a child. That is why the divorce rate is so high for such couples. When married partners communicate about their grief, love thrives.

One *joy* Bob and I shared mutually was the sighting of other young women who looked like Patty. It was like having a physical vision of Patty again to remember her beauty and softness. On occasion if I thought the woman might think we were staring at her, I would simply say:"You remind us of our daughter." On one particular occasion, Bob and I were taking a lunch break from skiing at Taos, New Mexico. One waitress looked exactly like Patty, even her physical body frame. The significance of Patty earning college tuition funds by waitressing also struck a chord with us. When this waitress took her break, she was reading a book like Patty always did to use every spare minute to study. Needless to say, these moments filled each of us with a certain awe and wonder.

Another good: I can now publicize information about suicide. One month after Patty died and we had emptied her apartment, I had time to go to a daily mass at our parish. For the first time I met the new pastor who had arrived the day before Patty died. I identified myself, said our daughter was a victim of suicide, and gave him two articles on suicide by Fr. Ron Rolheiser, and the homily Fr. Brian gave at Patty's funeral. I mentioned these materials might come in handy in his line of work.

One week later I went to the same daily mass. After all the others left after mass and conversation, Father told me that three days after I had given him the suicide materials, a priest friend of his had become a victim of suicide. Father was crushed. He had been asked to give the homily at the funeral for the grieving parish up north. Father's eyes said it all as he told me this. He could hardly believe the sequence of how all this happened. I responded that it was the Holy Spirit guiding things. And I knew Patty was helping to coordinate events. Father asked for prayers to help him deliver the homily. In prayer, I asked Patty to help him. The following week, Father said he delivered the homily better than he had actually prepared it. Father and I had a discussion on how Patty did not change her nursing job and his priest friend did not change his parish as a possible solution. In our way of looking at things we would think: why not switch jobs? Even though we may not think like the victim, I also think we need to ask ourselves what if the events happening to them were happening to us? What would we do then? By making it more personal, we might understand their situation better.

I ask these above questions because a lady had said to me: why didn't Patty just change jobs and hospitals? Four months later her husband landed in the hospital over a similar job situation. Sometimes it is totally different when it actually happens to us. Especially in our economy, job switching is not very easy. And if a contract is involved with a bonus, as was the case with Patty, changing jobs can be more complicated.

In the above discussion we also have to be mindful that our brains do not function the way their brains did in their last moments. We are approaching their problem from the outside objectively, rationally. In their last moments they were approaching their problem from the inside subjectively, irrationally. Thus we do not understand why they saw no way out of their situation.

Another good out of this event: I now pray for people who have anxiety, panic attacks, and those who are victims of suicide and their families.

Being aware of our vulnerability has developed as we realize we could not help Patty. But God could. Maybe we don't like the way God helped her, but we are not the ones in control here. God is. We do not have the power. We are frail humans. As Job 22:21 says: "Agree with God, and be at peace; in this way good will come to you."

After looking at Patty as God's gift to us, I could dwell on how much God loved her. I could then imagine Patty jumping into God's arms as she was transformed on June 22, 2005. This perspective of *gift* came to me after our daughter Jeanne wrote us a thank you for giving her Patty as a sister.

How can we live our lives better in honor of our memory of Patty's precious life? We think we can do this by imitating her compassion for the least and the little. We have joined the Vincent de Paul Society, do home visits for the needy, and continue to donate to a Charitable Giving fund in Patty's memory. We invested Patty's money to be used for the needy. We try to serve and share with them. The clients we serve have had a great influence on us, helping us grow. Sometimes I wonder if Patty is hand picking them for us.

Some outcomes for us in the Vincent de Paul work are: acceptance of everyone, no exclusions, and enjoying people's differences and uniqueness.

God wants to touch our lives by this loss of Patty. My manner of praying has changed. My attitude is: *however you think it should be, God, because You see the big picture.* At times the numbness leads to a way of not thinking at all. One's mind moves beyond words into silence. It moves into mystery too deep for words. Martin Buber expressed it this way: "All suffering prepares the soul for vision."

Reality has set in. We have eliminated the ..."What if's....? We do not blame anyone. Such thinking solves no problems and only creates more problems. That kind of thinking will not bring Patty back.

The support I have found in Sacred Scripture has been phenomenal. Passages have the power to speak to us in whatever situation we find ourselves. It is truly inspired by God when we can read it so many centuries later and find meaning in our life experiences today. *Woodrow Wilson said: "I am sorry for men who do not read the Bible every day. I wonder why they deprive themselves of the strength and the pleasure."*

Our pain has become something to be proud of; it exhibits our love for Patty that lasts forever. Kahlil Gibran said it this way: "And ever has it been that love knows not its own depth until the hour of separation.... The deeper that sorrow carves into your being, the more joy you can contain."

The French artist, Renoir, said: "The pain passes, but the beauty remains." The pain has not yet passed, but it is different because I believe I have grown in trying to help others with this type of pain. The beauty, Patty's beauty, definitely remains and is not blurred. I have indeed learned that every present moment is precious and will never return to be relived. I must soak it up now, not waste it.

I can be happy knowing Patty has the peace she deserves to have. As a result, I should not cling to the past but open up to the present to become the person I've never been before, the person God wants me to be. Can I open myself to change and growth?

Our experience is teaching us to have an understanding of mental health issues. We find everyone exhibits some degree of mental baggage to deal with daily. We need tolerance and support for each other since we are all connected in this human community called the world. Publilius Syrus said: "Pain of mind is worse than pain of body."

We hope to change the world's view and understanding of suicide and mental illness. In looking at people's needs, whether physical, mental, or emotional, it is easy to see why St. Paul was right when he said that God has chosen the weak of this world to shame the strong. A dramatic experience of this happened to me about ten months after Patty died when I was planning a memorial card of Patty at a print shop. The lady helping me asked how Patty died. When I answered, "Suicide," she told me her life history of mental illness. She described the hard struggle from childhood to get on track after three attempts at suicide, the difficulty in finding the right therapist, and the correct combination of medications. Now she was living a good life, growing and getting educated for a better job. She spoke to me as an intimate friend, opening the window of my mind. I was very touched.

Truly I have to thank God for His support and providence in my life. God embraced me when Patty died. I did not need tranquilizers or pills. I am so grateful. I do not like the chemical effects prescription drugs have on the body and mind. I would rather shed tears when a wave of grief overcomes me. It is natural to weep over a tragedy. One should not be ashamed of weeping. In fact, I was proud of my husband who cried several times. We had a good reason to cry.

A realistic outlook on our own aging process has evolved through this event. Perhaps others would look at me and say: "You have aged since Patty died." Aging is a natural process. It is inevitable. It will eventually happen to everyone. With God's help, I will cope with aging. I am grateful to God for His assistance in leading me to helpful resources that provide insight, encouragement, and strength.

Another good we were taught: don't be blind to internal values that matter in life. Catch on to what is meaningful and what is meaningless. We can all be more gentle with life. Regarding what is meaningful and what is meaningless, I spent about four months studying the book of Ecclesiastes four years after Patty's death. I used the *NIV Application Commentary* by Iain Provan. I meditated on his translation of the original Scripture as well as his commentary on it. For me there was extreme meaning in the study. Be aware of what is not lasting. My hope is that others would find similar consolation in this book of the Bible.

After studying carefully the book of Exodus in the Bible this past year, I was reminded of the book title: *When Bad Things Happen to Good People*. I had to re-evaluate the word "bad." In the big picture of life, things really are *not* "bad." They only seem bad to us because they make us suffer. For a while life is very unpleasant because of certain events. But in the long run the events are not "bad" because they eventually lead us to grow, become a better person, and teach us principles of life that only suffering or sorrow can teach. My *grief* has been my teacher.

As I have mentioned previously in this book, one of my sorrows was that I could not be physically present at Patty's side as she made her transition, shedding her physical shell like a coat too shabby to continue wearing. I do believe God and Patty understood this and gave me the "sacred" summer of 2011. During that precious summer, I experienced the hospice care and deaths of two of my older sisters, Sister Anne and Sister Rose, School Sisters of St. Francis. I am grateful to their religious order that I was able to be present every day with Anne and Rose during their last days. So many people fear such an opportunity. They would never believe (until they experience it) how very precious such hours of vigilance by someone's bedside can be. And to be present at the transition moment is "sacred." I am sure Patty's earlier transition prepared me for these two deaths and made them such a unique religious experience for me. It was a *gift* to hear each Sister make their decision known to a doctor repeatedly to accept death rather than dialysis. We had all seen our oldest sister, Sister Mildred, suffer through dialysis. Anne and Rose, in their eighties, did not want to linger and suffer the way she had.

Anne experienced kidney failure before Rose did. She was very brave. For three months she sat up in an easy chair at night to sleep so she could breathe. Whenever she would lie down, the liquid would push against her lungs to prevent breathing. Her legs and ankles were very swollen with liquid. When this began to happen, Anne took her name off the "call" list to tend to sick Sisters during the night at the Motherhouse. However, she still played the organ for Mass (which she loved to do), at the Motherhouse right up to May 25th when she had to be hospitalized because she could no longer breathe in a vertical position.

Anne was in hospice care from May 26th to June 5, 2011. During this time, Rose was by her bedside every day and cried frequently. I'm sure she was thinking this would be how she would also die in a couple years because she also was in kidney failure. Rose had lived with Anne the last thirteen years after she had returned to the United States after forty years of missionary work in Costa Rica and Honduras. They were like two peas in a pod.

One of Anne's last days when she tried to fight back tears, I reminded her of my favorite Scripture verses: "Do not be afraid. I am always with you." I showed her my bracelet with these engraved words and told her I had been wearing it since Patty's transition. I took the bracelet off and placed it on Anne's wrist. She was still wearing it when she transitioned at the same hour of the day as Patty had.

Anne had taught Rose how to transition to the next stage of life because Rose followed with the same strength when it was her turn six weeks later. I felt very strongly that they could not bear to be separated. At the sacred moments of transition Rose's labored breathing suddenly became more shallow. This drew the three of us closer to her side to touch her, pray with her, and assure her she could go. We bid her farewell. The breathing stopped. After a brief silence, there followed two louder exhales. (I wondered if it was the sound of her lungs collapsing). We stood transfixed, still touching Rose, trying to absorb what just happened. We waited in silence before calling the nurse.

To review Anne's and Rose's lives and help sort and dispose of their possessions was a reminder of how awesome it is to have family. I can't help but ask: *would I have soaked up this hospice-death situation had I not passed through the grief of Patty's transition? Thank you, God and Patty, for this holy experience.*

The morning after Sister Rose transitioned, I was doing my usual morning exercise and meditation as these words flowed into my mind:

Rose's Spirit
Rose,
Remember us as you leave this desert
Attend God's banquet table with honor
You are *free* now to *fly*
no more injustice to balance
no more critics to counter
no more barrio visits
no more slackers to motivate
no more prison schools to organize
no more professors to in-service
no more boys to orientate
no more arts & craft shows to raise funds
no more adults to direct
no more body guards to keep you from harm
no more drug addicts to rehabilitate
no more murderers to educate
no more hurricanes to weather
no more surgeries to mend the body
no more cancer to fight
no more kidney function to worry about

no more wounds to heal
no more limits
But wait a minute!
Could we be overlooking your *Spirit* presence
which still bonds you to us
to guide us, to lead us, to direct us,
to rehabilitate us, to protect us
with even more of God's power
than your physical presence could ever accomplish?
Rose, continue your ministry to us now
as God's embrace makes you whole.
Savor God's peace.
Realize God's energy.
Enjoy resurrection!

Last but not least, I experienced a sharper awareness and appreciation of creation's beauty. I never tire of *sunrises and sunsets* opening up a world of vastness, a leap into infinity. I no longer take them for granted but marvel at their beauty and soak in their awesome wonder. The Universe speaks through moon watching and star gazing. Shooting stars exhibit bombs of light like missiles in the night. When I see these wonders, I ask myself if Patty is setting them off for me. Gardening (see Chapter 11) helps me see the simplest of life as valuable and powerful. A realization of the preciousness of all forms of life becomes evident in outdoor work. An appreciation of rain and its power has developed in me. The complete double rainbow over our house was a vivid painting to be remembered forever in the enlarged photo our neighbor took of it. The balance of creation is at work as the rabbits dig their burrows in our flower garden, eat away at the balloon flowers and yarrow, and sit still among the ceramic bunnies for camouflage. The voles and mice are not to be undone as they root around eating insects and bugs out of the soil. My admiration goes to the variety of birds that visit the garden and eat the seeds out of the flower they are sitting on. Our flowers are natural bird feeders with no mess. The birds are the original acrobats, clinging to the bent flower stem while pecking the center seeds out of the flower. They actually help plant new growth by strewing the seeds in new places. Bird watching is easily a distraction in the morning. Their perfect pitch songs create great music to accompany my work. The wind lends its grace to the scene by bending and swaying the flowers while pushing the butterflies in bouncing swirls from flower to flower. The variety of bees is astounding. They are so busy and do not want to be interrupted. In winter the deer enter the garden in the snow to eat the rose bush stems I leave for them when no other food is available near the end of winter. On occasion raccoons leave tracks in the snow and mud. The hawks and turkey vultures help balance this life as they fly overhead watching all the ground activity. This abundance of life and the taking of life exhibit creation's cycle of life and death. Why does it seem so understandable for these forms of life but so mysterious when we see it in the human life cycle?

> *John 16:6-7 "Because I have said these things, you are filled with grief….it is for your good that I am going away." Was it for our GOOD that Patty went away?*

CHAPTER 11

Gardening as Psychotherapy

"Those who do not know how to suffer, do not know how to hope ….The patient sower, who entrusts the seed to the earth and the sun, is a person of hope."
Yves Congar (French Theologian)

As a gardener for some thirty-seven years, I have been aware that each kind of plant has different needs just like humans do. It is amazing how many analogies naturally come to mind. Each type of plant thrives in a particular location where it receives the correct amount of light and where the kind of soil has the right nutrients and proper drainage. This also applies to humans who need enlightenment to live, the right environment (soil), nutrients that feed the body, mind, and spirit, and proper hydration provided by a balance of time, activity, and solitude so one thrives rather than being overwhelmed.

My husband is the master vegetable grower. I am the master flower and shrub grower. During the days of numbness that followed Patty's funeral, I was so grateful for the miracle of rain that kept all our new landscaping alive at our new home. After a few weeks as we adjusted to organizing and removing Patty's possessions from her apartment, I was able to spend some hours each day caring for the garden again. As I did so, my eyes were dramatically opened one day as I transplanted some annuals into patio pots. I used special fertilizers to add to my watering can so that the new plants would not be so shocked in their new location.

As I did this in 2005, I applied this experience to human living. In real life we forget how traumatic a change of environment or change of job or "changes" of any kind can be on our life systems. Patty was very affected by change. She had difficulty psychologically before entering the change arena. Anxiety would build up because she thought she would be inadequate, e.g., before entering first grade after a good year in kindergarten, she said, "But I don't know how to read." We told her that's all right; you will learn how to read in first grade. And she did; she totally fell in love with reading.

During the last two months of Patty's life, she experienced too many transplantings that were sources of shock to her life: changed apartments (one mile from work to fourteen miles from work); changed from the ortho-med floor at the hospital to surgery; changed from working nights to working days; changed from sleeping during the day for one and a half years to sleeping at night; changed from not having nursing classes in the previous hospital position to a new regime of surgery classes which would last nine months. All these changes were shocks to her life. And I can't believe I did not suggest she get some help to cope with the changes. I did have the experience of 2001 with her anxiety and depression (Chapter 4), so I should have been more aware and alert to her needs.

As I have learned to move plants around the garden to find their ideal growing environment, I am conscious of how similar Patty's life was to these fragile plants. Some plants have had to be moved to better drainage areas. Some died because a big rock was one foot below and the roots had no place to grow. Some plants withered because of too much sun and others because of needing more sun. Some hot days the patio pots had to be moved to the shade to prevent leaf burn. I try to be attentive to what they need as I should have been attentive to Patty's needs. The plants provide the opportunity for me to tend life and growth, marveling that what I do does not make them grow. God does. Just how God makes them grow is really a mystery. Even though science can observe what helps growth, science is not the source of the growth. Mark's Gospel clarifies this mystery in 4:26-27. "It is as if a man were to scatter seed on the land and would sleep and rise night and day and the seed would sprout and grow, he knows not how." The principle of gardening illustrated here is: we do not control the growth or cause the growth. God does. The same applies to humans. We do not control humans and their behavior. We can only do our best to assist their growth, support them when they are in need, and listen with compassion, making suggestions. We cannot force a certain outcome with an individual because each of us has free will. We have to learn to let life grow where it will.

As winter leaves its traces of debris, the analogy with Patty's transformation on June 22, 2005 is very evident. Cleaning up all the mess and burning dried perennials is reminiscent of cleaning up her apartment for the next renter and picking up the pieces of our lives after they were shattered by the sudden loss of Patty. The spring season with new growth and longer daylight hours is a constant trigger to remember Patty's rising on her side of life.

Right after we celebrated the first anniversary of Patty's funeral, I planted two patio pots of coleus. After about a week, I noticed one plant was missing. What on earth happened to it? Did an animal dig it out? I moved all the leaves of the remaining plants and found the small plant hiding under the broad growth of a taller coleus. It had been stunted under the shade of the neighboring plant. I had placed it too close to the root of the taller plant. It was not going to grow there. So I dug it out and transplanted it to a spot where it had its own space and light. On the way back to the garage to put my tools away, a light went on – wow! That's what God, the Master Gardener, did with Patty. She had been struggling like the coleus, not receiving growth light while she was overshadowed by the mask of anxiety. God saw Patty was invisible in the mire, covered with frustration and depression, and anxiety. God saw her pain and her struggle to survive the overpowering emotional stresses of life. So God transplanted Patty to the next stage of life where she has space and gets light (God's light). Now God's light grows her roots independent of others crowding her and covering up her beauty. As I wrote this story in my journal, I felt the experience of the transplanting was teaching me how Patty's life is thriving, that she still loves us, ministers to us, and touches our lives every day. I wrote: "Oh, Patty, I miss you! I love you! Help me. Bring me peace and acceptance."

Shortly after the first anniversary of Patty's transformation, we drove by the farm we had moved from two years before. It was being demolished. All the mature trees were lying flat on their sides. They had not been hauled away yet. I photographed them. My heart pounded a bit, seeing all this destruction. I felt especially sad looking at seven trees along our old driveway that we had planted when I was pregnant with Patty. They had grown from eighteen inches to ten or eleven feet. They were all lying parallel to each other on the ground, gorgeous evergreens cut off very close to the ground. My mind could not help compare them to Patty lying on the ground on June 22, 2005. It reminded me that nothing is lasting. We have to let go because eventually we lose everything except God.

About a month before we celebrated the second anniversary of Patty's transition from this stage of life, I planted some coleus plants in shady parts of the garden. About two weeks later, they were dying and I could not figure out why as I had fertilized and watered them properly. When I dug them up, each of them had a fabric wrapped around the root system and the tiny little plants were not strong enough to break through the tough fabric. It made me immediately think of an analogous situation that I felt impacted Patty's brain when she was a baby. When she was eighteen months old she had a seizure due to a rapidly developing fever. She was hospitalized and for two weeks was given liquid phenobarbital, a barbiturate. A year later it happened again, followed by another two weeks of phenobarbital. After Patty's death, I read in suicide materials how barbiturates given to mothers giving birth had an adverse effect on their babies. Here we were giving the barbiturate directly to the baby. This terrified me and I believe this drug had an effect on Patty's brain and could have been a cause of depression in her life. We will never know for certain, but I cannot help but think that the drug may have acted on her brain the way the fabric hampered the roots of my plants.

Just as I have experimented with plants and flowers in various locations, I have also experimented with certain seeds that the wind blew in from the neighbors' gardens and from the fields and woods in our area. It has been fun to allow something to grow, not knowing if it is a flower or a weed. I began to adopt the policy of: if it wants to grow here and if it looks pretty, it stays. So there is some freedom to the arrangement of my garden. Some flowers other people might call weeds, but I think they are pretty and fill in the flower beds like a huge outdoor bouquet. I believe my free style garden is a symbol of Patty's free spirit. It represents Patty's desire to grow "where" she wants to grow. And I do believe she is doing just that in her resurrected form. Patty chose life on the other side/the next stage. I must let her go: to grow where she chose to go. One of my college classmates (an artist and musician) sent me a sympathy card in which she wrote: "Patty is now blooming on the other side of life."

Another reminder of Patty's blooming happened on the second anniversary of her transition to resurrection. My husband and I had traveled over to the site where she became a Spirit. The spot is located outside the apartment building and there are nice benches on which to sit facing Lake Michigan. I reverence the area because it is where a sacred thing happened, Patty's transfiguration. On that day, June 22, 2007, my husband and I sat on the bench and I opened up Gunilla Norris's book: *A Mystic Garden*. This book had been a great source of meditation for me. Whenever I had the opportunity, I would reflect on one page at a time. That day I opened to the next page and the title was "Blooming." I read it out loud. It was so appropriate speaking of the fullness of blooming and eventually the petals falling to the ground, calling it "the free fall of fulfillment" offering us the wisdom of "blossom and let go." This carried great meaning for us and demonstrated once again: *there are no coincidences*. We were sitting in silence meditating on these words when our daughter and her boy friend came up behind us. This was the only time she had come to this spot on June 22nd.

On the next Mother's Day, our daughter gave me a t-shirt saying: "Gardening is cheap therapy and you get tomatoes." Other than our vegetables, our garden surrounds our house except where the garage doors are. This makes me think of the garden of Paradise in Genesis, especially when I did a detailed study of it in Metro Bible Study a short time ago. Our lecturer emphasized the theme of "living trust" in our relationship with God and how humanity is constantly trying to cooperate with God's restoration of Creation. My rabbit plaque reminds me: "Remember the beauty of the garden for there is peace." My garden work is my effort to turn the world into the Genesis Garden of Eden again. Our garden that God has provided for us in our new location is a symbol to me of God's providence for us. It surrounds our house that God definitely provided for us in our retirement. The circumstances of our being able to build this house literally fell in our lap. We did not search for the opportunity. During the process of construction, God was definitely running the show. The beauty we see outside is only a small piece of Creation and the wonder of our Universe. We marvel at this wonder of Creation and try not to take it for granted. In my morning prayer, the garden becomes one of those ordinary things I am grateful for daily.

Three years after Patty's transfiguration, I had to tie up and bind the bottom split stem of a large zinnia plant. The wind and weather had torn it vertically below a large branch. When I wound a nylon cord around the stalk in two places to hold the two halves together, the cord only kept the stem from breaking off completely. The sheared inside of the stem was still exposed on each half. I photographed this broken stem because it reminded me of our family "being broken apart" by Patty's transition from this life. We were torn open, sheared, split, fractured by the traumatic experience. We have tied up our brokenness, hold together our scars, but a branch is still missing. We will always see the difference between the "before" and "after" picture. However, just as the zinnia continued to grow above the breach and bloom beautifully all summer so we go on with life in spite of our emotional upheaval. We, too, can still grow, flower, and bloom above and around the fracture. We know the scar will always be there, but it does not have to destroy us. It symbolizes Patty's presence in a different way than the world acknowledges, a spiritual presence we value. But make no mistake: the identity of our family is forever changed. The journey through grief will last the rest of our lives. It is a journey on which we can distinguish more clearly what is important and what is trivial, what is of value and what is meaningless.

The above example of the broken zinnia, makes me think of a quote from Rabbi Menachem Mendel of Kotzk: "Nothing is more whole than a broken heart." Patty's heart was broken in her panic on June 22, 2005. Emotionally she was broken. Physically, her heart was smashed and yet her heart was "more whole" than our blind human awareness can understand/perceive. I, too, can become more whole when I search consciously "my brokenness." Why? Because when I am "broken," I realize how dependent I am on God. He provides my wholeness. Then I will be stronger just as a broken bone knits and becomes stronger than before it was broken. Our family, too, will be stronger as we navigate through our grief. Recently I read this poem on a plaque to reinforce this idea:

Our family is a Circle of our strength.
With every birth and every union, the Circle grows.
Every joy shared adds more Love.
Every crisis faced together makes the Circle stronger.

Every time I accidentally knock off a fresh flower or accidentally step on a plant as I water or pull weeds, I twinge or hurt inside as it reminds me of a young person dying prematurely: Patty dying at age twenty-six. But then I am reminded of Abraham Lincoln's words: "It's not the years in your life that count; it's the life in your years...." Patty did live a very full twenty-six years. We are grateful to God that He gifted us with Patty. He allowed us to participate in her creation. He made her grow, but allowed us to tend and nurture her.

Sometimes analogies or parables cast a negative light on shallow roots, but I have found several positives about plants with shallow roots. Three plants of this type I have discovered are goose neck, yarrow, and woodland morning flowers. In draught conditions they may wilt, but when watered, recover immediately and look great. The other advantage they have is that they grow well over rocky or gravel type soil. That has been my experience around our patio where the construction workers were too generous with the gravel when laying the cement. The yarrow grows there making a beautiful perimeter border. Its shallow roots never reach the gravel. The shallow roots of the goose neck and woodland morning flowers seem to help them spread marvelously to fill in the garden spaces. Applying these assets to human lives, "shallow" is not always bad. For instance, if one is uprooted from a neighborhood because of a transfer, it helps not to be too attached to the location or the people so one can re-root in another location to spread and thrive there. It could be analogous to adapting quickly and being able to live in places that the average person cannot. Those of us experiencing grief, have to release our hold on the past and be flexible enough to live into the future, finding new ways to share our gifts with others even though we experience devastation. To arrive at this stage of resolution, we cannot stay rooted in our suffering. We may have to move and wander a bit in the desert. Exodus makes a point of this as the people escape from their slavery and wander in the desert. Our grief is a desert we wander through to escape being enslaved to it. If we keep moving, we will function again in a "Promised Land" provided by God.

Another interpretation of "shallow" for humans could be that some individuals are very sensitive because they are not thick skinned. Their feelings are close to the surface. Such persons, (like Patty), are caring, compassionate, and empathetic because they are not hard hearted. They wear their heart on their sleeve. They are usually very good listeners.

Another asset of the goose neck plant is that when its leaves get brown edges when needing water, it will recover when watered and the brown edges will disappear. But astilbe plants that thirst for water and show brown edges of drying out the leaves will retain the brown edges after watering because the leaf surface is very thin. Each plant recovers or does not recover according to its nature. This is also true of grievers. Some heal/recover after a reasonable amount of time and patience. Others will show signs of the pain of grief longer. Every griever is different because of their upbringing, their previous experiences, their love relationships, their education, their spiritual belief system, their personality, and their grip on reality. And that is all right. We are all different. It is unfair to say people have to fit a certain profile when dealing with their grief. One thing I am sure of is that we should all help each other heal after being struck with grief.

Droughts also can teach the griever. When the earth is dry, we realize our dependence on God for the miracle of rain. When the garden and grass are parched and browning from lack of rain, we find ourselves begging God for the right amount of gentle rain to nurture creation. After hours and days of watering to keep things alive, our hearts are grateful when we receive an inch of gentle rain. On my birthday or Mother's Day, I consider rain a gift. I am always in awe of how plants and shrubs grow by inches right after a rain. It is indeed a miracle we rarely recognize. As Jeremiah 2:13 says: God is a "spring of living water." After we experience desert conditions of drought, we finally understand God as "living water." In our spiritual lives, we are dry and even dead without God's living water satisfying us. Certainly when experiencing grief, I cannot imagine healing without God's life-giving water. For me, God's living water was available in Scripture. References for passages I meditated on in grief are listed in Chapter 9.

God, our Master Gardener taught another lesson this last growing season during our drought. Our tomatoes were a testimony on how we are to adapt to life day by day. When the drought came, the tomatoes had to rely on our watering them instead of getting natural rain. They grew tough skin. Amazingly when the tomatoes were added to soup, the tough skins disintegrated, not like other years when the tender skins cooked into rolled tough scrolls. These tomato skins really knew how to adapt to drought and cooking – most unusual. Can I do the same? Can I adapt to drought in my life? Can I cooperate, work with, and grow when life events heat up the temperature to wither me?

In addition, the tough tomato skins saved the tomatoes at the end of the growing season after we had two hard late frosts. Our tomatoes survived both frosts, were picked, ripened fully and were delicious – no soft spoiled parts. We have never experienced that in our thirty-seven years of growing tomatoes. Is there a lesson for me here? Can I survive cold shoulder treatment, frosty hard-hearted comments, and that silent glance that says it all? Can I be myself and always do what is right and fair even when it hurts to do so?

Another opportunity droughts give me: the chance to practice the "weeds and wheat" parable. While the parable illustrates why it is good to allow the weeds and the wheat to grow until harvest, I do that for several reasons: 1) during droughts those weeds actually shelter perennials from the burning sun by providing shade; 2) sometimes the weeds bloom into gorgeous flowers. Several early weed prospects I had turned out to be perennials I later saw on sale at a nursery. One of these plants turned out to be "liatris" or "kobokl" or "kobold." The common name is "gay feather." It developed into a thick clump and is spreading around the garden by its seeds.

This last discussion on weeds and flowers is like a parable teaching equality of human beings. So often we peg people in our minds and assess them by status or judge them morally as good or bad. By joining the Vincent de Paul Society and doing home visits for those in need, we are trying to get over that bias and see all people as equals. Instead of labeling them as weeds because they made poor decisions and got in a bind, we listen to their stories and find ways to help them.

As Gunilla Norris says in *A Mystic Garden*, there are so many invisible things going on in gardening. Just as there is invisible growth under the soil so the garden has an invisible influence on the gardener. We, in turn, are tilled, changed, influenced by our external garden activity: the planting, weeding, watering, fertilizing, pruning, separating, transplanting, dead heading, picking worms and bugs, spraying for mites, cutting down and cleaning up last year's growth in spring, disease control in fall, placing bark for water retention and protection, extra winter protection for delicate shrubs and roses. All these gardening activities have a mirror activity within the gardener for personal growth. We can apply each activity above to growth and disease control within. This is best done on an individual basis, finding where we need to prune, separate, plant, weed, etc. All these activities teach patience and flexibility. As we wait for garden growth, we learn patience with our own foibles and faults. As our garden fills in over the years, we learn to *"let go"* and accept God's providence one day at a time. We begin to accept God's timing, not ours. Gardening teaches us to accept *"what will be."*

A gardener experiences many of the frustrations of the farmer. But one must persevere in watering, weeding, and maintaining the garden as the season heats up, dries up, and the harvest struggles with bugs, disease, and maturity of fruit and food. This struggle in nature's garden can be compared to a human's challenge to handle and accept the death of a close family member such as our daughter, Patty. As the years roll on, I am like the Canaanite woman in Matthew 15:21-28, begging everyone not to ignore suicide victims in our midst. I am challenged to persevere like the Gentile woman of Syrophoenician origin in Mark 7:24-30. I persevere in my belief of God's mercy for suicide victims. I hope and believe that all is well, God is good, and faith will bring me home. I persevere in my sureness of resurrection for all of us. Just as I water and weed my garden, so I have to tend to my grief, my family, my faith, my character, my relationship with God. There are spiritual weeds to deal with and obstacles to step over or move away. As I water my garden, I remember there is nourishing water in God's Word and Sacrament.

Elizabeth Barrett Browning said this for those who see:

> *Earth's crammed with heaven,*
> *And every common bush a fire with God,*
> *But only he who sees takes off his shoes;*
> *The rest sit round it and pluck blackberries.*

The final new tree in our Garden of Eden at our new home was a hydrangea tree planted by our landscaper on June 22, 2005 in the morning. It became our symbolic Tree of Knowledge when Patty died that very day at five-twenty in the afternoon. I then knew more of life than I wanted to know. All of my life experiences had prepared me for this moment.

- Growing up on a farm made *birth* and *death* visible concepts.

- Being raised in a family of eleven made relationships important to me.

- Priest molestation in grades six, seven, and eight and again at age twenty-four taught me to be *forgiving.*

- My five years of temporary vows of poverty, chastity, and

obedience gave me a *spirituality* for which I will forever be grateful. Spirituality not only teaches one to look beneath the surface but also teaches the *surrender* that ultimately brings *peace*. It is my foundation that helps me find God even in desolation and sorrow.

- The ecstasy I experienced in child birth revealed to me what real interior *joy* is. I marveled at the *miracle* before me.

- Loving my husband and two daughters as the *center* of my life instilled relationship *love* that overflows into the abstract invisible Spirit world.

- My thirty-five years of teaching seventh, eighth, and ninth graders taught me frankness, honesty, and fairness in life.

- Being a mother *changed* me as a teacher.

- The suicides of one of my eighth-grade students, a fellow teacher, and a neighbor *opened* my mind to tragedies.

- In my retirement, grief ministry was *preparatory.*

- My meditative study of Scripture for the last thirteen years in Metro Bible Study proved to me that *God* still *acts* today in our lives.

- This has been my *annunciation journey.* Now seven years after Patty's transformation, I say with resolve: *"Be it done to me according to Your Word."*

Epilogue

"In a very real sense, the writer writes in order to teach himself, to understand himself, to satisfy himself."
Alfred Kazin

This reality book is intended for suicide families and friends if and when they need it. I have tried to be honest and forth right with the facts. Have I given definitive answers? No, because I don't believe humans have the answer. There is too much mystery that surrounds human misery and suffering. As some people express it, life is living the question or accepting the unanswerable. Two truths that suicide does witness to humanity are: 1) sometimes we do not do enough for our fellow human beings; 2) sometimes we cannot do enough for our fellow human beings.

My goal is to open a world of thought/vision for those experiencing suicide's aftermath. I hope our family's story illustrates that we can control *how we respond* when tragedy strikes unexpectedly. I have attempted to map my own grief, hoping it will help others grieve in their own way. "We make a living by what we get. We make a life by what we *give*," (great-aunt Alnette's notebook).

At one time I thought my mission in life was finding the love I experience with my husband and two daughters. But now I expand my purpose to channel that love to families who think life is over because of the suicide of a loved one. Perhaps this book can give them some hope to know that in time with some support they can function again and still accomplish some good in the world. Despite the fact that closure is a dirty word when we lose a child to suicide, we can face the truth and think of others to heal our wound.

Since I challenged the church in parts of this book, I wish to add here my new hope in the election of Pope Francis on March 13, 2013. His posture of humility when he appeared on the Vatican balcony and asked us to pray for him edified me. On Holy Thursday, he was the Servant of the Servants of God when he washed the feet of prisoners. He walks the talk when he rides the city bus and opts not to live in the fancy Pope's apartment. Is trust being restored?

In the winter of my life, my personal story has "come out" of the exile "world of suicide" to freely express my thinking and help others achieve a certain peace of mind. I am still wandering in the wilderness of suicide knowledge, but I will not be confined to it. I want to be "out there serving" others, proving there is life after suicide. I hope this book is pregnant with Patty's Spirit, guiding, nurturing, prodding, nudging, sheltering, and directing all who suffer the grief of suicide.

Please conclude with me that death is misunderstood.
Death is meant to be a wonderful transcendent experience.
It should not be feared.
We should embrace it in the same way we celebrate the birth of a child.
Like childbirth, death-birth can be messy.
Words such as euphoria, ecstasy, and exhilaration should describe it.
Thus every funeral becomes a celebration of a life.

"What we have done for ourselves alone dies with us; what we have done for others and the world remains and is immortal."
Anonymous

Bibliography

Bozarth, PhD, Alla Renee, *A Journey Through Grief* (Center City, MN: Hazelden, 1990).

Care Notes, Multiple titles dealing with death, suicide and loss (St. Meinrad, IN: Abbey Press).

DePaulo Jr., MD, J. Raymond and Leslie Alan Horvitz, *Understanding Depression* (Hoboken, NJ: John Wiley & Sons, Inc., 2002).

Gibran, Kahlil, *The Prophet* (New York: Alfred A. Knopf, Inc., 1927).

Huntley, Theresa M., *When Your Child Dies* (Minneapolis: Augsburg Fortress, 2001).

Hyde, Margaret O. and Elizabeth Held Forsyth, MD, *Suicide,* Third Edition (New York: Franklin Watts, 1991).

Jamison, Kay Redfield, *Night Falls Fast, Understanding Suicide* (New York: Vintage Books, 1999).

Kubler-Ross, MD, Elizabeth, *Death, the Final Stage of Growth* (New York: Simon & Schuster, Inc., 1975).

Kubler-Ross, MD, Elizabeth, *On Life after Death* (New York: Random House, Inc. 1991).

Lewis, C.S., *A Grief Observed* (New York: Harper Collins Publishers, 1961).

Moore, James W., *When Grief Breaks Your Heart* (Nashville: Abingdon Press, 1995).

Norris, Gunilla, *A Mystic* Garden (New York: Bluebridge, 2006).

New Revised Standard Version: Catholic Edition, *The Catholic Youth Bible* (Winona, Minnesota: St. Mary's Press, 2008).

New International Version, *Life Application Bible* (Wheaton, Illinois: Tyndale House Publ., Inc., And Grand Rapids, Michigan: Zondervan Publishing House,1991).

Oliveira, Jacquelyn Frances, *The Case for Life Beyond Death* (Elm Grove, WI: William Laughton Publishers, 2000).

Robinson, Rita, *Survivors of Suicide*, Revised Edition (Franklin Lakes, NJ: New Page Books, Division of the Career Press, Inc., 2001).

Rosof, Barbara D., *The Worst Loss: How Families Heal from the Death of a Child* (New York: Henry Holt and Co., 1994).

Shea, John, *The Spiritual Wisdom of the Gospels for Christian Preachers and Teachers, Year A, Year B, Year C,* Three volumes (Collegeville, MN: Liturgical Press, 2006).

Smolin, C.S.W., Ann and John Guinan, PhD, *Healing After the Suicide of a Loved One* (New York: Simon & Schuster Publishers, 1993).

Trickett, Shirley, *Anxiety and Depression: A Natural Approach* (Berkeley, CA: Ulysses Press, 2001).

Trickett, Shirley, *Panic Attacks: A Natural Approach* (Berkeley, CA: Ulysses Press, 1999).

Walton, Charlie, *Twelve Faces of Grief* (St. Meinrad, Indiana: Abbey Press, One Caring Place, 1998).

Library Books

Doka, Kenneth J., *Living With Grief–After Sudden Loss.*

Dolce, Laura, *Suicide,* 1992.

Marcus, Eric, *Why Suicide,* 1996.

Wrobleski, Adina, *Suicide: Survivors* (A Guide for Those Left Behind).